Ramsden Balmforth

The New Reformation and Its Relation to Moral and Social Problems

Ramsden Balmforth

The New Reformation and Its Relation to Moral and Social Problems

ISBN/EAN: 9783337295608

Printed in Europe, USA, Canada, Australia, Japan

Cover: Foto ©Suzi / pixelio.de

More available books at **www.hansebooks.com**

THE NEW REFORMATION

AND ITS RELATION TO

MORAL AND SOCIAL PROBLEMS

BY

RAMSDEN BALMFORTH
(LAON RAMSEY)

LONDON
SWAN SONNENSCHEIN & CO.
NEW YORK: CHARLES SCRIBNER'S SONS
1893

CONTENTS.

CHAP.		PAGE
	PREFACE	vii.
I.	THE DECAY OF ORTHODOX BELIEFS	1
II.	THE FUTURE DEVELOPMENT OF RELIGIOUS LIFE	29
III.	THE SANCTIONS OF MORALITY IN THEIR RELATION TO RELIGIOUS LIFE	59
IV.	THE SANCTIONS OF MORALITY	85
V.	THE NEW REFORMATION AND ITS RELATION TO SOCIAL PROBLEMS	113
VI.	THE TRUE TEACHERS OF THE WORKING CLASSES	131

PREFACE.

THE first four chapters of this book originally appeared in the pages of the *Westminster Review*, over the pen-name—"Laon Ramsey." Chapters V. and VI. are now printed for the first time.

The last chapter may not appear to have a very direct connection with the other parts of the book, but, to the writer, it is perhaps the most important section, dealing, as it does, with ideas and principles, the realisation of which must necessarily have a profound influence on the moral and religious thought of our time. What has been well termed "The New Reformation"—a phrase for which I am indebted to Mrs. Humphrey Ward—must include not only the *inner* religious life of man, it must include the whole of life; for religion, whether it take the form of art, or moral endeavour, or philosophic research, being the bed-rock on which the higher life of man is founded, if that foundation is in anywise altered, the whole structure must necessarily be affected by the change. It is recorded of Plotinus that he died with these words on his lips—"It has been my aim to bring the God which is in man into harmony with the God which is in the universe." This, too, is the aim of the New Reformation, and it is an aim which can only be realised by bringing the influence of religion to bear on the outer life—the life of the citizen, the workman, the organiser of labour, the artist, the economist, and the politician. So that the New Reformation has its economic and political side as well as its religious side. It is really a war of the spiritual faculties against the degrading influence of debasing materialistic conditions,—"a war," as Dr. Clifford puts it, "a war of mind against the brute force of matter. A war which will end the fight for poverty, so that we may begin the fight with ignorance, with vice, with inexact thought, with low ideals, and base aims." It is only by such a Reformation, mightier than any which has preceded it, that we can bring the life of man into harmony with the life of God.

The essays on the future development of religious thought and life do not in any sense pretend to be an accurate forecast of that development. They are simply a natural attempt on the part of a mind nursed in scepticism to search out the truth and to formulate for itself a constructive religious faith,—and in this matter one mind may be taken as the type of thousands in an age which is marked by the spontaneous dissolution of orthodox beliefs. If the book should aid any other searcher, not, indeed, by presenting to him a faith ready-made, but by throwing one ray of light upon the pathway of human knowledge, and thus making "the skirts of darkness narrower," its purpose will have been fulfilled.

R. B.

HUDDERSFIELD, *April*, 1893.

THE NEW REFORMATION.

CHAPTER I.

THE DECAY OF ORTHODOX BELIEFS.

"IF there is one thing which a comparative study of religions places in the clearest light, it is the inevitable decay to which every religion is exposed." These words, taken from the Introduction to Professor Max Müller's *Chips from a German Workshop*, will doubtless come with a shock to the mind of the orthodox reader, for it is one of the signs of the remarkable influence which religion exercises over the human mind, that while all things else are admittedly in perpetual change or transformation, religion itself is said to be the one exception to the universal law. Every believer looks upon his own religion, or, at any rate, the fundamental doctrines of his religion, as the veritable "Rock of Ages"—the one eternal, unchangeable Truth. The above quotation from Professor Müller, altered so as to apply to anything other than religion, would sound but the stalest of platitudes; applied to religion, it strikes the note of contention which so often gives to religious controversy an especial bitterness, for there can be nothing more distressing to the mind of the devout worshipper than the suggestion that he is worshipping at a false shrine.

To the student of religions, however, this fact stands out clearly and distinctly—that the religious life, in all its forms and aspects, is subject to the law of evolution. To him, it is not only the physical universe—from the tiniest weed to the stateliest oak, from the sands on the sea-shore to the granite hills—which is in a state of perpetual transformation, but also the thoughts and feelings of the human mind, the latter being subject to the universal law perhaps in greater degree than are the objects of the physical world, for the impressionable and sensitive mental states of man are acted upon by ten thousand "hidden suckers" which incline him now this way, now that, keeping his emotional, moral, and intellectual being—his mind—in continual flux.

And, as with the individual mind, so with systems of thought and religion; the law of evolution affects not merely each separate religion, but, through these, the whole of the religions of the world. The enormous influence which Judaism had upon Christianity is sufficient illustration of the latter point, while as to the operation of the law of evolution on separate religions, I need only refer to the development, or, indeed, the transformation, of Christianity itself. From the Galilean era, the primitive stage of Christianity, through the age of Gnosticism and the metaphysical schools, through the centuries during which

Christianity, under the form of Ecclesiasticism or Roman Catholicism, rose to the height of its power, and again through the period in which we see the rise and establishment of Protestantism and its off-shoots, we may clearly and certainly trace the development of the Christian religion. We may, indeed, point to certain eras and say: "There Paganism began to decline, here Christianity became the dominant religion;" but no man can lay his hand on any particular epoch and say: "There Paganism was extinguished, here Christianity was established." There is a slow decline of the one, a gradual development of the other. The methods of thought, the ceremonies, the practices, and the institutions of the one, assist in the evolution of the other, and the Christian religion is indirectly influenced by Paganism, just as we in the nineteenth century are influenced by Roman law and Greek philosophy. The thought of one age, in religious as in secular matters, is bound to leave its impress on succeeding generations.

This process of development may be clearly discerned in the vague unrest which characterises modern Christianity. There is a tendency to broaden theological doctrine; the interpretation of Scripture varies with the progress of knowledge—passages which were accepted as literal a generation or two ago being now looked upon as figurative or allegorical. Church of England ministers express doubts as to the truth and morality of certain of the Thirty-nine Articles; the doctrine of eternal torment, once vehemently upheld as a restraint on evil-doing, is now generally discredited. Even the most intolerant sections of the Church are influenced, perhaps unconsciously, by the liberal spirit of the age.

This change in religious belief is, however, too obvious to need further insistence upon. We are thus brought face to face with this most striking fact—that independent of the *form* which religion may take, there is a progressive continuity in the religious instinct and the religious life. Roman Catholicism in the Middle Ages attempted to break this continuity, to enchain the human mind to a fixed belief. It was an impossible task, as impossible, indeed, as to chain down the earth and release it from obedience to the law of gravitation. Development is an absolute necessity. If, then, there is a progressive continuity in religious instinct and religious life, it necessarily follows that on the decline of orthodox Christianity the religious life would still continue to manifest itself in other and superior forms.

There may be some, however, who, while accepting, or perhaps partially accepting, the theory of evolution as it affects religion, would demur to this conclusion; who would say that though there have been, and still are, differences in the manifestation of religious life, yet there can be but one true religion, and that this is to be found in all its fulness and perfection in the Revelation which God has made to man. To such objectors it is necessary to present a different argument; to show them that truth and goodness are not peculiar to any particular religion, or to any divinely-favoured section of humanity, but that these belong, in certain measure, to the whole of mankind. For religion, on its subjective side, is essentially a *striving after something higher*—wherever this is found, consciously or unconsciously manifested, there is the true religious spirit. And in most, if not in all, of the religions of the world, we find this element in varying degree. In Hinduism, in Buddhism, in Mohammedanism, as well as in Christianity, it is largely manifested. In the sacred books of each of these religions there are precepts which are not only of a kindred character, but which are identical in spirit and in meaning. A few examples will illustrate and enforce my argument. " He who cleaveth firmly unto God is already directed into the right way. Let there be people among you who invite to the best religion, and command that which is just, and forbid that which is evil."[1] " Verily God commandeth justice and the doing of good, and the giving unto kindred what shall be necessary ; and He forbiddeth wickedness, and iniquity, and oppression : He admonisheth you that ye may remember."[2] " Your Lord knoweth well that which is in your souls; whether ye be men of integrity : and He will be gracious unto those who sincerely return unto him."[3] " Whatever is in heaven and earth singeth praise unto God ; and He is mighty and wise. He is the first and the last ; the manifest and the hidden ; and He knoweth all things. He causeth the night to succeed the day, and He causeth the day to succeed the night, and He knoweth the innermost parts of men's breasts. Believe in God and His Apostle, and lay out in alms

---

[1] *The Koran*, chap. iii., Sale's translation.
[2] *Ibid.* chap. xvi.
[3] *Ibid.* chap. xvii.

a part of the wealth whereof God hath made you inheritors."[1]

Again, from the older religions of the East we have such passages as the following: "I will proclaim as the greatest of all things, that one should be good, praising only righteousness. Ahuramazda will hear those who are bent on furthering all that is good. May He, whose goodness is communicated by the good mind, instruct me in His best wisdom."[2] "We worship Ahuramazda, the righteous master of righteousness. We praise all good thoughts, all good words, all good deeds which are and will be done, and we likewise keep clean and pure all that is good. O Ahuramazda, thou righteous happy being! we strive to think, to speak, to do, only what of all actions may be best fitted to promote the two lives (that of the body and that of the soul)."[3] "We worship righteousness, the all-good, all that is very excellent, beneficent, immortal, illustrious, everything that is good."[4]

"If, friend, thou thinkest thou art self-alone, remember there is the silent thinker (the Highest Self) always within thy heart, and *he* sees what is good and what is evil."[5] "There is one eternal thinker, thinking non-eternal thoughts; He, though one, fulfils the desires of many. The wise who perceive Him within their self, to them belongs eternal life, eternal

---

[1] *The Koran*, chap. lvii.

[2] *Zend-Avesta, Yasna*, xlv. 6. *Vide* Haug's *Essays on the Religion of the Parsis*, p. 163. Second edition.

[3] *Yasna*, xxxv. 1, 2, 3. *Vide Ibid.*

[4] *Yasna*, xxxvii. 4. *Vide Ibid.*

[5] *Laws of the Mánavas*, viii. 92. *Vide* F. Max Müller's *India: What can it teach us?* p. 74.

peace."¹ "Varuna is merciful even to him who has committed sin."²

"Avoid doing all wicked actions, practise most perfect virtue, thoroughly subdue your mind; that is the doctrine of the Buddha."³ "Deeds that are hurtful to oneself, and deeds that are wrong, are easy to do; deeds that are beneficial and that bring happiness, they are difficult to do."⁴ "The reward of virtue is happiness; he who has made that his goal will speedily find perfect rest and Nirvána."⁵

The reader will perceive the similarity between these passages and many in the Old and New Testaments. I may observe, however, that I am not here invidiously comparing the religions of the East with Christianity; indeed, I am quite willing to admit that every religion should be judged as a whole rather than by its separate parts, that the unity and harmony of the doctrines promulgated should be taken into consideration in determining the worth and the originality of any religious faith. What I wish to insist upon is this: that the central principle of the ancient religions is really identical with that of Christianity. In each, there is the same indestructible element of belief in the triumph of good over evil. The powers of light are opposed to the powers of darkness; Indra (the god of the sky) to Vritra (the demon of night);

---

[1] From the *Upanishads*. *Vide Ibid.* p. 248.

[2] *Rig-veda*, vii. 87, 7. *Vide* F. Max Müller's *Chips from a German Workshop*, vol. i. p. 41.

[3] *Dharmatráta*, translated from the Buddhist Canon, by W. W. Rockhill, p. 133.

[4] *Ibid.* p. 135.

[5] *Ibid.* p. 154.

Ormuzd (the principle of good) to Ahriman (the power of evil), just as the idea of God is opposed to the idea of the Devil, good to evil, in our own day. It is immaterial to our present inquiry whether the doctrine taught is that there are two opposing principles of good and evil, or that there is only one force in Nature, the various manifestations of which produce good and evil accordingly; the result is the same—there is a striving to accept and perpetuate the good, and to reject and destroy the evil.

This similarity, which is so apparent in a general view of the religions of the world, also manifests itself in the lives of the best of the adherents of each religion. Sakya-Muni, in the purity, devotion, and renunciation of his life, is, like Jesus, typical of sublime saintliness; Marcus Aurelius stands far higher than any of the Christian sovereigns of modern times —foretoken, let us hope, of the time when philosophers shall be kings; and many of the ancient philosophers were imbued with as high a moral spirit as were the Christian saints. The truth is, there can be no equitable division or comparison based on difference in religious doctrine. The attempt which has lately been made to divide mankind into the spiritual and the non-spiritual, the natural man being regarded as spiritually dead, fails at the very outset by the absurdity of the assumption. Wherever there is conscientious thought, or conscience, there is the germ of spirituality; wherever there is a striving after righteousness, there is the basis of the religious life. The outward working or example of this spirit may be denominated differently by different individuals; one may term acts of goodness the "grace of God" manifested in one's earthly life, another may say that good actions spring from "a love and a reverence for humanity." There is only a difference of names. The real feeling underlying the various terms is the same, yesterday, to-day, and for ever. The scientist, in investigating natural phenomena, may name and classify the laws which govern these, but though the names may alter as experience widens, the underlying force ever remains the same. The biologist, in examining the diverse forms of life and the functions manifested in each, classifies and names the various forms and functions, but though the classification may vary and the name change, each function still continues its manifestation. So the theologian, in analysing the ideas and motives which occupy the human mind, builds up from these his creed and doctrine, and imagines that he has formulated the true religion; but the creed and the doctrine pass away, while the underlying principles and motives which impel to moral and religious endeavour still remain and influence mankind. Theology is changeful, evanescent; the religious spirit is permanent, and inherent in the human mind. There is a substratum of universal truth and goodness which is independent of all theological dogmas.

Thus do we find, by a reference to the intellectual and moral growth of man, that the religious life, in one or other of its forms, is essential to humanity; that the striving after truth and goodness is not confined to any particular sect or creed, but is, in varying degree, an element of all.

Seeing, then, that Christianity is but one amongst

many forms of religion, all of which are founded on a principle or sentiment which is inherent in the human mind, my task is largely simplified, for it resolves itself into, first, a consideration of the disintegrating tendencies of modern thought on orthodox beliefs; second, an outlining of the *necessarily* religious and moral effects which would follow the decadence of orthodox Christianity. The sincere and earnest Christian, whose mind has been imbued with the belief that Christianity is the true faith, that it contains within itself the divinest moral sanctions and the potentiality of all good, may well be dismayed at the thought of its decay. He may, indeed, conscientiously ask himself whether man, deprived of the consolations of that religion which he has so long held sacred, will not sink into immorality and dissoluteness; whether, in such a contingency, our Christian civilisation will not decline and fall as previous civilisations have fallen. But if he can be brought to see that every form of religion is subject to the law of evolution; that, with the loosening of the traditional bonds of morality, there arise, with the concurrent intellectual reformation, higher motives and sanctions; that the moving, or dynamic, or relative element in human life, is constantly striving to place itself in harmony with the ideal good, then an important step is taken towards catholicity of thought. That moment the theologian tacitly, if not willingly, admits that there is a moral and emotional basis for all religions; that, on the decline of any particular faith, the general law of development would still hold good, and that man, instead of slipping his moral moorings, would cling to the higher and nobler sanctions which are the possession of our common humanity.

Before proceeding to the next division of my subject it will be well to again draw the attention of the reader to the important fact already insisted upon, a fact which is, indeed, implied in the very word "evolution," and which it is imperative to bear clearly in mind in discussing the future development of religious thought, namely, that the immediate substitution of one religion for another is an impossibility, but that the religious life of one age is bound to bear the impress of that of preceding ages. Although this is really a truism, and is implied in all that I have yet written, its importance and bearing cannot be too strongly insisted upon, for orthodox people have a tendency to regard opponents as the apostles or expounders of a new religion in contradistinction to the old, and exclaim: "If you think you have a better religion than ours, formulate your faith, and let us examine your creed so that we may see if it will bear comparison with ours;" as though religion were a ready-made article, whereas it is really a *growth*. It is this difference between manufacture and growth which is the real root of the difference between theology and religion. Theology deals with the supernatural and its relation to the human; religion deals with the human in its relation to the ideal and to the eternal mystery of which human life is a part. While theology stereotypes the supernatural, anatomises God, and fixes the ideal, treating these as an architect treats his plans of some magnificent building, religion regards the Supreme Power as, in its essence, unknowable, and leaves room for the expansion and growth of the ideal. True, religion has a theoretic basis, but this is not to say that it is necessarily theologic, any more than to say that a theory of art or of music is theologic.

This, then, is the fundamental difference between the theologian and the truly religious man—the one formulates his infallible creed and lays down a fixed plan of salvation; whilst the other, regarding religious life as a growth, seeks to direct that growth aright, to free it from noxious weeds, to purify the highest instinct in man's nature from the degrading influence of the superstitions of preceding ages.

Here, then, we are brought to the all-important question—If there is a basal element or principle which is peculiar to all religions, what is that principle? Or, with special reference to Christianity, what is the underlying principle on which it is built, and which will remain when the Christianity of the schools has passed away? By due consideration of these questions we shall be able to obtain a clear idea as to what is essential and what is non-essential to true religion, and we can then forecast, with some degree of precision, the probable consequences which will follow the decay of theological creeds, and the consequent stronger growth of the religious instinct.

I have already defined religion as *a striving after something higher* and it is the recognition of this all-pervading "something" which is the basal element of all religions. No matter what name is given to it —" God," " Nature," " The Unknowable," " The Beyond," "The Eternal, not ourselves, which makes for Righteousness "—this something is recognised by all civilized beings. And even amongst the uncivilized there is a similar though narrower conception:

> " Lo, the poor Indian, whose untutored mind
> Sees God in clouds, or hears Him in the wind."

This, then, is the foundation of the religious sentiment —the recognition of, and, in various forms, sympathy with, the Invisible. It is this resistless, this overpowering sense of the reality and permanence of the Invisible which forms the basis of man's conception of the Supreme, and it is essential that we obtain some idea as to the further evolution of this conception, for, as this varies, so will the religious life assume new phases. Hitherto, the popular conception of God has been narrow and limited—a vague notion of an extraordinary Being with human sensibilities and powers largely magnified. Of course, this conception varies according to the mental constitution of each individual, and becomes wider in proportion as the mind is susceptible to the influence of culture. But in this conception of the Supreme, whether held by the adherent of the Salvation Army or by the orthodox dignitary of the Church, there is one and the same inherent defect; that is, that God is supposed to be an all-wise and all-powerful *Person*, who has arranged the life of mankind according to a certain plan, and who will ultimately reward or punish His children according as they believe or disbelieve in the Divine authorship and wisdom of this plan. This is the cardinal defect. Out of this there flow, as, indeed, there must necessarily flow, numerous other defects which vary in the same measure as the creeds of the different sections of the Church vary; defects which are part of the assumed divine plan—the doctrine of the Incarnation, the Trinity, the Atonement, the plenary inspiration of Scripture, Justification by Faith, and numerous others pertaining to the orthodox theology. It never seems to occur to the upholders and defenders of this plan, that, after all, it may not be the expression of the Divine Will, but merely the outcome of their own imagination, or of the imagination of their forefathers, as to how the Divine Will *should* manifest itself—their own pet idea as to what the plan of the universe should be. And the principal recommendation of this imaginary scheme of Divine government is said to be its preciseness and definiteness of character, thereby giving to man a body of doctrine according to which he can frame and control the conduct of life. But when we come to examine this scheme of theology, we really find that *for us*, one of its chief characteristics is its indefiniteness, an indefiniteness arising from the initial step—the anthropomorphic presentment of the Deity. Of course, in a certain sense, all presentments of the Supreme must be anthropomorphic. But the anthropomorphism of the orthodox theologian and that of the adherent of the Church of the future differ in this —that whilst the anthropomorphism of the one is *essential*, or inherent in the conception (a Being with human powers largely magnified), that of the other is *accidental*, and is occasioned by the *inadequacy of language* in portraying man's conceptions of the Eternal. These anthropomorphic conceptions of the Deity must then, I say, be both indefinite and impermanent, varying with every individual and at different periods of life with one and the same individual. Indefinite, because the personality is bound to be vague; we are never quite sure how much of man and how much of God there is in the conception; there may arise, now and then, some doubt as to the wisdom and justice of certain parts of the "plan." And the conception is necessarily impermanent, because it is an attempt by man, the finite, the transitional, to give a fixed presentment of that which is infinite, eternal. It is an attempt to stay the onward, ever-developing movement of the intellect. With every change in the conditions which determine the growth of the human mind there must come corresponding changes in man's conception of the Supreme Power, and thus there is a continual transformation, a gradual rejection and re-creation of religious, or rather, theological systems, a making and an unmaking of gods. The popular theological conception of the Deity must, then, go the way of the ruder presentments which have preceded it. Like the barbarous conceptions of savage tribes, the beautiful and more refined conceptions of Pagan polytheism, and the still more ideal conceptions of the ancient religions of the East, this anthropomorphic presentment of the Supreme contains within itself the seeds of natural dissolution. The degrading familiarity with God, which is so prominent a characteristic of our popular theology, is therefore bound to pass away.

But though the Biblical presentment of the Deity is now tacitly rejected, at anyrate by the "masses," it may be said that the conception of the Supreme which is likely to obtain in the immediate future will still be that of a Personal Being, shorn of the barbarous attributes with which popular theology has hitherto endowed Him. If this be the case, then a wave of purified Theism will doubtless pass over the religious life of the people, and the Unitarian body may look for a great accession of strength. Of this, however, there are at present no great signs. Still, it may not be out of place to consider for a few moments whether the Theistic conception of God is a legitimate one, and whether it is likely to have a paramount influence on religious thought. This conception I take to be that of a "Supreme Mind and Will, directing the universe, and holding moral relations with human life," which means, of course, nothing less than an Infinitely Perfect *Personal* God. Undoubtedly, this conception of the Supreme is quite natural and legitimate *if it is in accord with the emotional instincts of the believer.* (Note, however, in passing, that it is the contention of this essay that the Theistic conception of God is not now in accord with the emotional instincts of a large portion of mankind.) From the emotional or the intuitional point of view, Butler's argument in the *Analogy* is of no use—all depends on the state or quality of the emotional feeling possessed by the individual. It is really a question as to how many straws will break the camel's back, or, as Mr. Brooke in *Middlemarch* would say, one may trust and believe "up to a certain point, you know." Because there are difficulties connected with the Theist's conception of Divine government—difficulties such as, for example, unmerited suffering, which is apparently at variance with the rule of an All-powerful yet Loving God, and the reason for which the sincere believer trusts will be made clear in God's own time; because there are these difficulties, I say, which the Theist overcomes by his faith in and reliance on the living God, that is no reason why he should be called upon by the orthodox theologian to accept further difficulties, which shock his moral sense—to believe, for example, in an Almighty Being who will consign His children to eternal punishment for errors in belief. The state of the Theist's emotional feeling may be such that he would look upon such a Being as an unnatural monster limned by a crude imagination, rather than as an All-wise and Loving God. So with the Protestant, the fact that he accepts the doctrine of the infallibility of the Scriptures, and overcomes the difficulties of his belief by leaving the meaning of doubtful passages to be made manifest in God's own way, is no reason why he should be called upon to accept the further difficulties involved in the doctrine of the infallibility of the Church. Where the justification for belief is purely subjective there is nothing more to be said. It is useless to argue against a person's beliefs if he tells you that he *feels* they are true.

All this is, of course, from the standpoint of the emotions, and emotion knows no logic. The Theist, however, as we are well aware, does not stop here; he must descend into the arena of controversy, and give a reason for the faith which is in him. He prides himself, above all else, on being "rational" in his religion, and so he has to settle with Bishop Butler on the one hand and with Herbert Spencer on the other. Let it be distinctly understood, however, that the moment the Theist so descends into the arena of controversy, that moment does he leave the domain of religion for the arid subtleties of the dialectical fencing-room. And however fascinating to a certain order of mind dialectical exercise may be, it is too anarchic in its results, too fond of finding justification and proof for itself, to be prolific of divine religious life. Religion, on the other hand, manifested either in thought or in feeling, scorns proof, or rather, it is a proof in itself. It is not merely prolific, it is creative, intensifying the vital element in man, purifying Passion, ennobling the Ideal, exalting Enthusiasm, transforming, transmuting, transfiguring Life. Of the one, the hair-splitting and the casuistry of Scholasticism may be taken as the type; of the other, the life of a Christ, a Buddha, a St. Francis d'Assisi.

This, then, is the cardinal defect of Theism, that it loses its potency in the process of proof and justification. "He who excuses himself, accuses himself." Dr. Martineau in his work, *A Study of Religion: its Sources and Contents*, says:—" By religion I understand the belief and worship of Supreme Mind and Will, directing the universe and holding moral relations with human life,"[1] and he forthwith proceeds to give justification of this conception of religion in two large volumes, which cover a large portion of the field of metaphysical research. Despite all Dr. Martineau's eloquence, however, we close the work with a feeling of sickness of heart at the thought that religion should

[1] Introduction, p. 16.

require such portentous justification. Religion needs no such justification—irresistible and majestic in its sweep, it flashes forth its proof in the radiance of its martyr heroisms. The antithesis of the religious instinct is the sceptical instinct; and scepticism—the real sceptical instinct—never is, never can be, enthusiastically religious. But let us beware of the misuse of terms. With scepticism towards lower forms of faith, there may be allied a passionate fervour for nobler ideals, a profound reverence for higher faiths, and those whom the world has been ready to label with the name of "sceptic," have often been men and women of finest religious feeling.

Independently, however, of the fact that the positing of a Personal Deity leads the rational religionist into the debatable land of metaphysics, and that Theism thereby loses its potency as an effective religious faith, there is a further reason for supposing that it will never again touch the hearts of the people. I have already said that Theism is not really satisfying to the emotions of a large portion of mankind. This assertion will doubtless appear strange to those who are accustomed to place reliance on an infinitely loving Father, and who, in this thought of trust and reliance, find consolation for the wearied spirit and balm for the troubled soul. Yet the absence of trust is a quite natural consequence. Before a Being can inspire trust and reliance, the character and the workings of that Being must be such as will spontaneously generate these qualities in the hearts of his children. A kind and loving father, who entwines his child in his arms and fills its breast with a sense of his sustaining power, gives to the little one a natural feeling of trust and love which causes it to cling to its parent to the end of life. But a brutal father, who is callous to childish affections, who cares not for the welfare of his little one, who wreaks cruel vengeance upon it for childish misdeeds, and fills its baby brain with continual apprehensions of his brutal fury—such a father can inspire no love and no trust. So with the Infinitely Perfect God of the Theist. The works of Nature are said to be the manifestation of God's infinite power and wisdom, and we are told to contemplate this manifestation of infinite power, the wonder, the beauty, the bounteousness of Nature, and give praise and glory to God. So we do. But when we remember that under every fair-seeming leaf there is a miniature world of woe; that the bird which at one moment thrills us with its song, may, at the next, hold a writhing worm in its jaws of death ; that the dusky veil of night, with its setting of brilliant gems, is the pall of millions of ephemera ; that every tread of our foot in the fields may leave scores of dead and maimed victims ; that the continuance of healthy vitality in one half the animal creation means the quivering death agony of the other half ; that, finally, this inconceivable amount of misery and suffering is not a mere accident in Nature, but is the very woof and framework of existence, the whole universe groaning and travailing with pain ; when we remember these things, I say, and are told by the Theist to give thanks and praise for *this*—we are dumb. Neither will the doctrine of Compensation suffice—this merely softens, it does not remove, the jar on our emotional feelings, for no compensation can wipe out the wrong of *unmerited* suffering. Thus, for us, the All-perfect, All-powerful, yet Loving *Personal* God of the Theist fades into nonentity—we *cannot* believe, because of the very excess of our emotional feeling.

But this line of argument will lead us to Atheism, it may be said. Not at all. Neither does it leave the existence of God "an open question." We are still conscious of the illimitable presence of the Supreme. In the words of Herbert Spencer: " Amid the mysteries which become the more mysterious the more they are thought about, there will remain the one absolute certainty, that man is ever in the presence of an Infinite and Eternal Energy, from which all things proceed." We know and feel that there is a *tendency* which makes for righteousness, and it is to this that we are willing to give praise and glory. But beyond this we cannot be called upon to go. We will praise the Good, but do not ask us to bow down to Evil. More of this anon, however, when we come to consider the reformative influences at work on religious life.

It may be objected by both the Rationalist and the Agnostic, that I am here laying too much stress on "mere" emotion, that all such questions should be decided from the standpoint of Reason. By all means, let us appeal to Reason where such appeal is necessary, but let us not neglect subjective or intuitional experience. There has of late years been such an enthroning of Reason that one may be excused for thinking that the cultivation of the emotions is in danger of being neglected, and it may not be unwise to enter a protest, however feeble, against such a policy; though, after all, the emotions form such an imperishable portion of man's being that perhaps no permanent harm can arise from this temporary neglect. We are continually being told that religion must be "verified," that it must rest upon a "demonstrable basis," that it must have its warrant in "objective realities." There is, indeed, no need nowadays to insist upon appeals to the reasoning faculties for the decision of religious questions, rather is there a need to insist upon such a wise cultivation of the emotions as will impregnate the religious sentiment with a more puissant vitality. However much the scientific method has accomplished in undermining the leading tenets of the Christian faith amongst the cultured classes, with the great mass of the people emotion has been the most potent factor. The belief in the doctrine of eternal torment, for example, has passed away, not through the historical and critical researches of Biblical scholars impugning the accuracy and authenticity of New Testament records, but because the moral sense of the people has revolted at the doctrine. The fear sometimes expressed by devout people that religion will die away with the decadence of the old faith is most puerile, from the very fact that emotion, from which religion springs, is an indestructible element of man's being.

Nevertheless, by this transformation of religious thought, we are brought face to face with a very serious problem—not merely with the *question*, Does a Supreme Personal God exist? but with the *fact* that for the great mass of the people no such Being does exist. We have been building on a false foundation. The "Time-Spirit" is at work, and to attempt to destroy its influence by dialectical exercises on metaphysical questions would be a waste of energy. The results arising from this negative attitude of mind are serious, and must have a pernicious influence on the religious life of the people. Take, for example, the custom which is the natural outcome of a belief in a Supreme Power—*i.e.*, prayer or supplication. It is quite natural for one who is in great stress and danger to appeal to the One with whom he conceives he has some direct personal relation; it is, indeed, quite natural for the mind in which this conception of a Personal God exists to appeal for the satisfaction of even material wants. And thus we have in our churches those materialistic prayers for rain, for fair weather, for deliverance from plague or from famine, or even for victory in battle; or, in other words, a pious entreaty that this personal yet omniscient and loving Father of all may allow one portion of His children, who may be filled with a lust for conquest and dominion, to mercilessly slaughter some other portion of mankind, who may have the misfortune to be smaller in number than the first-named portion, and who may therefore be in greater need of the protection of an all-powerful and infinitely loving Father. But with the passing away of the old theological conception of a personal Deity, the custom and form of prayer must have a corresponding change, and it is gratifying to notice that in the Church itself such prayers as these are gradually coming to be looked upon as really blasphemous in their nature—an insult to the Providence whose interposition they invoke. The mind of man has become so thoroughly impressed with the uniformity of Nature that all appeals for the disturbance of that uniformity are rightly looked upon as useless. Thus the offering of prayer for the satisfaction of material wants will soon become a thing of the past.

As to the further changes which the custom of prayer is likely to undergo, this must be left for consideration at a later stage; here I wish only to emphasise the fact that, by insisting so strongly on the doctrine of the Personality of God, and by inferring that the custom of prayer depends upon this crude conception of Deity, the theologians themselves have unconsciously done much to undermine the very spirit on which prayer is founded. And a similar danger attends the relation which the Bible has hitherto borne to the intellectual life of the nation. "Destroy the old conception of a personal God," says the orthodox Christian, "and you depreciate the value and lessen the significance of the Scriptures." What reliance may be placed on this statement Matthew Arnold has well shown us. But the evil has been done and the danger is upon us. The "masses" read the newspaper instead of the Bible, or, at best, their reading is composed of a great deal of newspaper and very little Bible; but perhaps it is better that it should be so than that they should read their Bibles wrongly. Compare the influence of the Scriptures to-day with their influence, say, three hundred years ago; I mean in the intensity of that influence rather than in its extent. Then, to the great bulk of the people, the Bible was the only literature, and though they read it wrongly and gave it a false interpretation, yet it gave to them vivid conceptions of duty, grand ideals, and high purposes, and by these they were enabled to bind tyrant kings in chains, and, with hail of fire, scorch out of the land the immoral theory of "the right divine of kings to govern wrong." But the Bible gives us no such vivid conception of duty to-day, not because it does not possess the power of giving such conceptions, but because we have lost our base,—the people having been taught that the Bible is the revelation of a Personal Deity, the personality having vanished, they have, not unnaturally, come to regard the revelation as a myth, and disregard it accordingly.

Thus we see how the disintegrating forces at work on religious life accumulate and gather strength. And the great need of the time is to change these disintegrating forces into reformative forces; to render possible a deeper, a truer expression of the religious spirit in man; to make all that is best in Christianity aid in developing that spirit; to revivify and intensify our conceptions of duty, and to make those conceptions the basis of a more resolute endeavour for the attainment of a high ideal of moral and social life. To do this, it is necessary that we admit to ourselves and recognise the fact that our conceptions of the Supreme have undergone, or are undergoing, a vital change. We need a readjustment of religious thought to the wider knowledge to which the human race has attained. There cannot be the least doubt that the break-up of the old faith will extend to the very foundation of religion—for the conception of the

Supreme is the ground-idea of religious thought. And this is where the danger lies. But it is a danger which arises, not from intelligent disbelief in a Personal God, but from indifferentism, from unconscious Atheism, if I may so term it. The people have been taught to expect so much from the "divine plan" of orthodox theology—the beneficence of a Personal Providence who would hearken to the prayer of the faithful, the remission of sins through Christ, the materialistic heaven, and the still more materialistic hell—that, with the loosening of the bonds of traditional belief, there may be some danger of a lapse into selfish indifferentism. Should this danger become a reality, however, there need be no fear of selfishness and indifferentism remaining permanent. The religious instinct in man is so strong, the desire to follow the truth and to act justly towards others, has, generally speaking, become so inherent in man's nature, that it is almost impossible there can be any real and permanent weakening of these qualities. There are periods in human history when religious life seems devoid of potency, but this is no proof that religious life does not exist—it merely flows through unseen channels, gathering strength to burst forth with irresistible power at later periods. Thus, the religious life of the immediate future must be the fruition of the religious life of past ages. The loftier Paganism produced a type of character beautifully, divinely heroic; Christianity came and gave to that type the perfecting touch of saintliness, and Paganism, which was individualistic, became transformed by the new doctrine of the brotherhood of man. Slowly, gradually, the divinely heroic was lost sight of; the wealth, the exuberance, the genius of philosophic life was ready to perish in the formalism, the casuistry, of Scholasticism. Out of this apparent barrenness, however, sprang the Reformation, or, to speak more broadly, the enthusiasm, nay, the exaltation, of that reforming spirit which culminated in the fiery earnestness of the French Revolution. Again came the swing of reaction, and now, in these latter days, pure Christianity has lost its potency in the slough of a sordid, degrading industrialism. But again, I say, this is no proof of the permanent decadence of the religious spirit. There are signs that mankind is reawakening to a sense of its position and duty, and it is in this reawakening that the religious life must again burst forth, blending the Stoic ideal with the Christian ideal, the divinely heroic with the saintly; giving to us once again the charm, the majesty of the golden age—men and women living in the grand, the god-like style.

> " Alone, self-pois'd, henceforward man
> Must labour! must resign
> His all too human creeds, and scan
> Simply the way divine!"

Thus it will be seen how strong is the logical continuity in the manifestation of religious life. A continuity as strong as, because it is part of, human life itself. It is perhaps difficult for the mind to realise that the myriad experiences of past ages must exert their influence in each individual life of to-day, yet we cannot doubt that this influence, arising out of ancestral feelings, habits, prejudices, prepossessions, dogmas, does indeed mould the life of each generation. And it is this adamantine chain of continuity in thought and life which gives us such great hope for the future, and prevents us from regarding the decadence of orthodox Christianity as the decadence of religion itself. As long as the human mind is constituted as it is, so long will it continue to ponder the old problems, so long will the insatiable curiosity of man prompt him to dig and delve at the old unplumbed mines. So long, too, will his labour be productive of the same results—systems of philosophy and systems of theology which differ only in symbol and in name. And the systems of philosophy wane and pass into oblivion, the systems of theology die away, and, like the Pagan women of old, we weep for our dead gods and bury them in shrouds woven out of dim, indefinable longings and hopes. But, as a bird renews its plumage, our ideals rise again, robed with a grander radiance, a diviner light, and our minds become endued with a larger hope, a firmer faith, a higher conception of duty, a clearer perception of the forms in which duty should manifest itself. The old shrines crumble to ruins, and we build for ourselves new temples. Let us take care that the Temple of the Future be reared with loving hands and steadfast hearts, the remembrance of which shall nerve the worshippers therein to more heroic action, to saintlier life.

CHAPTER II.

THE FUTURE DEVELOPMENT OF RELIGIOUS LIFE.

ONE of the most striking features of the mental unrest which characterises our age is the co-existence of a profound moral earnestness with a deep unsettlement of religious convictions. The manifestation of this moral earnestness—which is exbibited in every department of life, intellectual, social, and political—affords indisputable proof that the progressive tendencies of our time are not imbued with the purely sceptical instinct. A due appreciation of this fact would, of itself, allay the fears of those who are inclined to believe that in our modern thought and life there is a permanent decadence of the religious spirit. For the sceptical instinct is of the intellect, and springs from a desire, a longing, for intellectual freedom, while the moral earnestness, the moral fervour which characterises our age—more potent, far, than the sceptical instinct—is of the conscience, an aspiration for the realisation of divine justice. It is this which is stirring society to its very depths, and which, in its dim aspirings, ever yearns for communion with the divine. Hence the puerility of the fears of those who would have us believe, that on the decline of any particular faith or doctrine, the religious spirit is in danger of decay. No; dwarf the religious instincts to-day with the crudities of a barren theology, or cut them out with the knife of a cold rationalism, and they will rise in the human breast to-morrow with renewed strength and beauty. Yet it may be true that the effects of our moral earnestness, in so far as that earnestness is not a part of our religious life, may be to some extent—to what extent it is impossible to determine—rendered nugatory by the uncertainty attending our religious convictions. The triumphant success of the Puritans in the first half of the seventeenth century was due to the fact that they had a vivid conception of a divine standard of truth and justice, and cried in clarion tones of assured triumph: "Let God arise, and let His enemies be scattered! Like as the mist vanisheth, so shalt Thou drive them away!" But the religious spirit of the nineteenth century has no such conception. The old idols are breaking, the old conceptions are fading. The breath of the "Time-Spirit" is upon them; yea, those who would fling hot denial at my words are unconsciously swayed by the spirit of the age, and, ere long —nay, even now—their lips falter and their hearts fail as they murmur the old and meaningless formulas. We yearn for authority, and yet know not where to find it. And again and again arises the mighty, agonising cry: "Give us Objective, Eternal Truth," and again and again is the tortured spirit driven in, in upon itself, wearied, baffled, to the terrible anguish of that isolation of soul wherein the passionate heart vainly yearns for communion with the Divine. Oh! that the Eternal Verity would rend its veil of mystery and shine with starry clearness into our tear-dimmed eyes! And yet, the human spirit heroically and sublimely faces the emergency, and, with Promethean grandeur, defies despair. Though it may lack the personality of the Divine, it still possesses the glorious vision of the Ideal, and maybe in our secret aspirings we feel that in the measure in which we *perceive* the true Ideal, in that measure do we perceive God, and in the measure in which we *realise* the Ideal, in that measure do we realise the Will of God.

If, then, we can do something, however little, towards a resettlement of religious convictions, towards establishing a surer basis of religious thought, rendering possible a truer expression of religious life, so that we may feel that we are working for grand realities rather than for dim phantoms, so that our moral earnestness may be fruitful rather than futile, then our labour will not have been wholly in vain. Let it not be thought, however, that in tracing the probable development of religious thought, and in seeking a common bond of spiritual union, I have any intention of formulating or describing with any degree of precision the doctrines and the ritual which shall compose the religion of the future. True religious feeling is too spontaneous, too intensely sympathetic, too genuine and healthy a growth to be outlined and portrayed in mere mechanical fashion. But the tendency, the trend—if I may so use the word—of religious thought and feeling may be plainly discerned by anyone who will take the trouble to compare the thought and literature of to-day with that of even two generations ago. It has now become almost a platitude to say that the spiritual life may be attained in many and diverse ways, that the Supreme may be approached by paths unknown to the theological mind. To Shakespeare, the drama was religion; to Shelley, poetry. To the artist, beauty is religion; to the martyr, heroic endeavour. To these, and such as these, the consummation of life, of religion, is the perfectness of their work. But to those of us who are neither poets, nor artists, nor martyrs, and whose minds are cast in the common mould, some unifying Ideal is needed, an Ideal which shall unite us in a common bond of fellowship. The religious life, the religious spirit is, at bottom, always the same, and our points of agreement may be deeper, may be of more importance, than our differences. If, then, we can but find a point of agreement on such a grave problem as the true conception of the Supreme, if we can but formulate a standard of belief which shall accentuate our agreement instead of embittering our differences, surely those differences will be one step nearer a solution. "God," wrote Sebastian Frank, as quoted by Richter in *Levana*, "God is an unutterable sigh lying in the depths of the soul." How simple that is, and how true! A longing for the Ideal, aspiration for the true and the good, there is the Spirit of God manifested. And yet our friends the theologians will object that the definition is merely poetic. Well, and are not all our definitions of God poetic, figurative, from the very nature of the case; language "thrown out," as Matthew Arnold says, at certain grand realities which we cannot fully comprehend? And the theologians themselves, in their better moments, admit this. They allow that to furnish a complete definition of God is an impossibility, and they quote with approval the fine language of Zophar and of Job. "Canst thou by searching find out God? Canst thou find out the Almighty unto perfection? It is as high as heaven; what canst thou do? Deeper than hell; what canst thou know?" "Lo, these are parts of His ways: but how little a portion is heard of Him?" Would that our theologians always manifested the same spirit.

I have already said that the conception of God is the ground-idea of religious thought. How important, then, it is that we obtain a true conception of the Supreme! How necessary it is that we get rid of those crude ideas which represent God as a superior kind of man, with exactly the same notions as to the plan on which the universe should be worked as we ourselves happen to possess; and that we get rid, also, of those metaphysical definitions, the non-acceptance of which is said to imperil one's immortal soul! The truer our conception, the better shall we be able to form for ourselves an affirmative faith for the conduct of life.

What, then, is that conception of the Supreme which is likely, in the future, to form the basis of religious thought and life? Is it not furnished by the existence of that Eternal Power, whatever name we give to it—Nature, Force, the Absolute, or God—the manifestation of which is clearly visible in the universe around us? For a metaphysical conception of God we have no need to go in search. Here, around us and within us, the existence of this Power is plainly to be discerned, needing no subtle mental process for its recognition by the human mind, but verifiable by the simple evidence of the senses. And along with the manifestations of this Power, we may also note the *manner* in which it works—always towards the perfection of things; an apparently inherent tendency in the universe to produce and render enduring that which is good, and to destroy that which is evil; or, as Robert Buchanan finely expresses it:

"All that is beautiful shall abide,
All that is base shall die."

The definition nearest in accord with this higher conception of the Supreme is the one given by Matthew Arnold—" The stream of tendency by which all things seek to fulfil the law of their being;" or that more popular one—"The Eternal, not ourselves, which makes for righteousness." The latter, however, is open to some objection, for the tendency towards righteousness, though active outside ourselves, is yet a part of, and within, ourselves. For man, indeed, the working of this tendency *within* him is really the most important business of life. I am aware that Mr. Arnold attempts to justify the phrase " not ourselves" by pointing to "the very great part in righteousness which belongs, we may say, to *not ourselves*." (*Literature and Dogma*, popular edition, p. 21.) But Mr. Arnold himself, a few pages farther on in the same work, makes a distinct concession to the idea to which I have drawn attention, by alluding to the Eternal Power, "in and around us, which makes for righteousness . . . . Conduct, righteousness, is, above all, a matter of inward motion and rule." So I think. And though this tendency to perfection or righteousness is indeed visible outside ourselves, yet the more we strive to strengthen that tendency within ourselves by inward rule and guidance, the more shall we be influenced by our conception of God, the more truly religious will mankind become.

Here, then, we have a conception of the Supreme Power which is in accordance with the phenomena manifested in the universe, and free from those metaphysical ideas of the personality of God, which, to many minds, involve so much contradiction and absurdity. "The Eternal which makes for righteousness." It is a conception which is easily realisable by the human mind, not, indeed, in its wholeness or completeness—for in this we should again be bordering on the realm of metaphysics, the ideas or concepts of the Supreme which elude complete formulation—but in its direct bearing on the life of everyone of us. It is a conception which can be brought home to the meanest capacity, while every increase of knowledge gives it a fuller and a deeper signification. "As righteousness tendeth to life, so he that pursueth evil pursueth it to his own death."[1] "Keep innocency, and take heed unto the thing that is right, for that shall bring a man peace at the last."[2] As the whirlwind

---

[1] Proverbs xi. 19.
[2] Psalm xxxvii. 38 (Prayer-Book version).

passeth, so is the wicked no more, but the righteous is an everlasting foundation."[1] Or the same thought expressed in the words of another religion:

> "Before beginning, and without an end,
>   As space eternal, and as surety sure,
> Is fixed a power divine which moves to good,
>   Only its laws endure.
> It seeketh everywhere and marketh all :
>   Do right—it recompenseth ! Do one wrong—
> An equal retribution must be made,
>   Though Dharma tarry long."[2]

But do not let us delude ourselves, as I am afraid Mr. Arnold deludes himself—or, if that is too harsh a term to use of so revered a teacher—do not let us assume, as Mr. Arnold assumes, either that righteousness *necessarily* brings the reward of happiness, or that this doctrine can always be verified in the life of every individual. True, *generally speaking*, righteous conduct may be said to bring happiness, and it is possible—nay, probable—that the martyr at the stake may be sustained by a serene and exalted felicity beside which our poor experience is as naught. But there can be no doubt that, on the other hand, right conduct does often bring pain and misery to the doer, and that wrong conduct does often, apparently, bring happiness in the shape of "mouth-honour," "troops of friends," and worldly wealth ; a poor kind of happiness, doubtless, but still a kind which often seems to give satisfaction to the possessor. Perhaps I cannot do better than quote Mr. Ruskin's words on this subject:

[1] Proverbs x. 25.
[2] Arnold's *Light of Asia*.

"Foolish moral writers will tell you that whenever you do wrong you will be punished; and whenever you do right, rewarded—which is true, but only half the truth. And foolish immoral writers will tell you that if you do right you will get no good; and if you do wrong, dexterously, no harm. Which in their sense of good and harm, is true also, but, even in that sense, only half the truth. The joined and four-squared truth is, that every right is exactly rewarded, and every wrong exactly punished; but that in the midst of this subtle and, to our impatience, slow, retribution, there is a startlingly separate or counter ordinance of good and evil—one to this man, and the other to that; one at this hour of our lives, and the other at that—ordinance which is entirely beyond our control, and of which the providential law, hitherto, defies investigation."[1]

But it may be said, "If it be that this doctrine cannot be verified in our own individual life, how shall we verify it?" And I reply, "If you want verification, look to the experience of the race, there you will find proof, ample proof, that righteousness tends to the happiness of mankind. But do not try to verify it by your own individual experience. You have no right to try to verify it in that way, no right to inflict pain on a fellow-creature for the mere purpose of proving whether pain will give *you* pleasure. The experience of the race, viewed as a story of human life, is sufficient; and as a subjective, intuitional reality, that experience, welling up in your own consciousness, gives additional incentive to moral endeavour." And if it

[1] *Fors Clavigera*, Letter xiii.

be further said, "Seeing that this doctrine cannot be verified in our own lives, *why* should we give our adherence to it and found our action upon it?" I answer again, "Certainly not *because* it may bring happiness in some future life. To do this is to reduce religion to a mere matter of bargaining, to imitate the ways of the spoiled child who is induced to perform its duties by the promise of a sugar-stick." But this is hardly the place to enter upon the serious question as to the sanctions of morality. Let it be sufficient at present to say, that as we have been told time after time that there must be room left for the exercise of faith, for the expression of the feeling of trust in, and dependence on, some higher principle, here is room for the exercise of that faith and that dependence. To the great majority of thinking people the proof is clear; one needs only to open one's eyes to see it. Of the minority, who cannot or who will not see it, and who will not have faith in the experience of the wisest and best of mankind—of such it can only be said that they are wholly and irrevocably "lost."

It will doubtless be objected that this conception of the Supreme, as a tendency which makes for righteousness, is but another form of Nature-worship, and that Nature, with her coldness, her passionlessness, her pitilessness, cannot command that reverence which is due to a personal deity. But this objection is based on a misconception. The works of Nature are but the manifestation of the inscrutable Power underlying appearances. What this Power is in its essence or in its totality we do not know; but this we do know, or, at any rate, this we are justified in asserting, that it moves towards perfection, and that, in its highest manifestations—that is, in noble types of human life—it reaches such an elevated form of expression as *may* be the dim reflection, as it were, of an Infinite consciousness. Let it not be understood, however, that I have any serious disagreement with the man who finds in an all-comprehending, harmonious unity, termed Nature, an object of reverence and of worship. We have surely passed the stage of quarrelling about names, and whether we call our Ideal " Nature," or " Humanity," or the " Eternal which makes for righteousness," or " God," matters nothing, so long as we recognise that the worthiest form of worship is the imitation of the God-like life, the devoting our energies to the realisation of the Kingdom of God on earth. I am aware that some even of the mildly heterodox school of thought are strongly opposed to what they would term the deification of Nature, as, for example, Dr. Martineau, who, in his most recent work, expresses himself emphatically against accepting Nature as a synonym for God. " Nothing can be more misleading," he says, "than to say that 'God is merely a synonym for Nature.' The attributes of Nature are birth, growth, and death ; God can never begin nor cease to be : Nature is an aggregate of effects; God is the universal cause: Nature is an assemblage of objects ; God is the infinite Subject, of which they are the expression: Nature is the organism of intelligibles; God is the eternal intellect itself. Cut these pairs asunder ; take away the unchangeable, the causality, the manifesting Subject, the originating Thought, and what is then left is indeed ' Nature,' but, thus bereft and alone, is the negation and not the synonym of God." "Nature, therefore, can never swallow up the supernatural, any more than time can swallow up eternity."[1] It would be easy for the Nature-worshipper to retort upon this, that Dr. Martineau is arguing upon false analogies; that to compare Nature and Time is to compare incomparables, Nature being eternal, Time fleeting—night passes into day, spring verges into summer, but the Eternal Mother remains behind. He would say that Dr. Martineau confuses the *order* of Nature with Nature herself. Is it, indeed, correct to say that Nature is born and dies, that it begins and ceases to be? Is the mind of a Shakespeare to be included in the " assemblage of objects ? " Is not the moral and religious life of man as truly a manifestation of natural life as is the growth of a tree? If not, where, in religion, does the natural end and the divine begin ? And what are the supposed manifestations of supernatural power— the trees springing into blossom, the fields bringing forth abundant harvest, the heavens showing forth the majesty and sublimity of the universe—what are these but the orderly manifestation of natural laws? And if it be said that the methods of Nature are cruel, that, for example, an earthquake shock which destroys thousands of lives, or a famine which destroys millions, is not a very pleasing exhibition of harmonious and orderly development, the Nature-worshipper may again retort that it is just such phenomena as these which render the hypothesis of a Personal Deity untenable, appearing, as to so many minds they do,

[1] *A Study of Religion: its Sources and Contents.* Introduction, p. 8.

irreconcilable with divine wisdom and goodness. For ourselves, however, we should be little disposed to disagree with Dr. Martineau if, by the term "God," he means the invisible Noumenon of which phenomena are the manifestation. In this sense it is idle indeed to talk of "cutting the pair asunder." But we know that Dr. Martineau means much more than this, and he must needs put God and Nature in striking antitheses. That there is something behind or underlying natural phenomena, and that this something may be termed "God" we affirm quite as emphatically as does Dr. Martineau, but not in the sense in which he would have it—that is, a Personal God who thinks and loves; that, at least, is not clearly provable. It is now too narrow a basis on which to build our religion. Let us, then, be content to say that there is a power in Nature, infinite and eternal, which moves towards perfection, but which, though persistent in consciousness, in its totality eludes formulation by the human mind. This attitude of reverent humility is, we are convinced, the true relation of man to the Supreme.

It may be objected that this conception of God cannot inspire that passionate devotion which, it is said, finds expression in the lives of those who cling to a Supreme and Loving Friend. To such objections the answer is clear. The saintliest courage, the divinest heroism, is that which is unsustained by any thought of personal sympathy; is, in short, that which stands *alone*. Reliance on a Supreme *Personal* Friend suggests too strongly "a lively sense of favours to come," in the shape of the happiness of the soul after death. But the soul which has no such reliance, which is willing to sink its individual chance of happiness now and for ever in its efforts after righteousness—that is the God-like, religious life, which needs no verification and no justification, but before which the uncovered multitudes bow in silent homage. Mr. R. H. Hutton, in his essay on Matthew Arnold, lays great stress on this supposed want of emotion in the new religious life, and, in referring to the emotion which is "to transform morality into religion," he goes even so far as to say that "without faith in [a Personal] God, plague, pestilence, and famine are more likely to touch immorality with emotion, than to touch morality with it." No, decidedly no. Rather is the reverse of this true; for with a transformation of faith, with faith in human endeavour instead of in an imaginative conception of God, morality would be touched with deeper, intenser emotion. With no faith in, and no prayer to, a deity who, with a wave of his magic wand, could stay the suffering from plague, pestilence, and famine, there would arise in the human breast a more heroic endurance, a sterner fortitude, a more compassionate heart, a sublimer faith—faith in the purity of the earnest heart, and the potency of the girded loins. Mr. Hutton makes the strange mistake—mistake unaccountable in so able, fair, and generous a critic—of confusing "emotion" with "joy." There is emotion excited by the alluring prospects of the Mohammedan paradise, with its gardens of delight, its goblets of flowing wine, and its beautiful houris; but what emotion! In Christianity the emotion is deeper and finer—"Father, forgive them, for they know not what they do" .... "into Thy hands I commend my spirit," was the cry of a demi-god! But the emotion is still finer and more intense in the stoicism of the future—a stoicism refined and exalted by its union with the highest ideal of Christian life, self-sacrifice— "No change, no pause, no hope," was the cry of a God. Prometheus, chained to ice-crowned Caucasian peaks, with the vultures tearing at his vitals, must always remain the highest type of heroic endurance. This, it will be said, is an impossible religion. Impossible for the great majority of mankind, doubtless; just as to live the life of Christ is impossible to ordinary mortals. But not impossible as an ideal towards which men may strive; and the measure of their striving will be the measure of their religious life.

"Will, then, the religion of the future," it may be asked, "change our emotions of joy into emotions of sadness?" "Hear my cry, O God; attend unto my prayer. From the end of the earth will I cry unto Thee, when my heart is overwhelmed; lead me to the rock that is higher than I. I will abide in thy tabernacle for ever; I will trust in the covert of thy wings." "The Lord is my strength and my shield, my heart trusted in Him, and I am helped; therefore my heart greatly rejoiceth, and with my song will I praise Him." "Take this from us," it will be said, "and you give us a religion of despair." Perhaps I may be allowed to interject here, that, independently of all emotions either of joy or of sadness, the primary question is one of truth, and we know that the reward of the earnest searcher after truth is pain, immedicable pain. Let us accept the burden unmurmuringly, and bear our cross manfully. Much, very much allowance must, however, be made for the period of transition through which we are passing. In the olden days, when men were ruled by tribal deities, the traveller, wandering far from the haunts of his childhood, would yearn for the protecting influence of his familiar Spirit; so, too, on the decline of Paganism, the Roman matrons would lament their lost gods, and turn with melancholy to the shadowy substitute of the Infinite One. So, to-day, the sense of loss occasioned by the decay of faith in a Personal Deity will create a feeling of sadness, which, whether temporary or permanent, is bound to leave its impress on religious life. But with the decay of faith in a Personal God there will arise nobler conceptions of the Eternal, which will, to some extent, compensate for this loss of affection. Love for a problematical Personal Deity will be transformed into love for man and for the Ideal Good, bringing in the end a more opulent affection, a diviner sympathy, a profounder spiritual life. But it is not for the orthodox Christian to upbraid us with a sadness naturally pertaining to the loss of holiest illusions, for the same sense of sadness is manifested in Christianity. It is reflected in the Psalms in passionate outpourings of the spirit. The poem of Job is instinct with the same feeling. It inspires some of the most sublime outbursts of the prophets; it is manifested in the life of Jesus, in the writings of Paul, of John, and in those of a host of devout Christians of later times. The dread of displeasing God, and so losing the divine favour, the sense of contrition and despair at possibly unforgiven sin, the thought of the few saved and the many who are "lost," all these add to the anxiety and despondency of the devout. Despite the alleged consolations of the doctrine of the personality of God, one must experience a feeling of relief on exchanging the more gloomy doctrines of orthodox Christianity for the comparative freedom and buoyancy of natural religion. Still, although I would be far from asserting that a morbid melancholy is the necessary concomitant of religious life—much more strongly, indeed, would I assert the reverse—I think it cannot be denied that at the root of all intense religious feeling there is a tinge of melancholy, and the higher the religion the more marked is this sense of sadness: compare, for example, Buddhism with Mohammedanism; a melancholy arising, perhaps, from the mere contemplation of the awe-inspiring panorama of Nature and of life, from the overwhelming sense of the littleness and loneliness of man compared with the immensity of the universe, from the terrible abyss which separates finite knowledge from infinite wisdom, from the deep and awful mystery in which, in any scheme of salvation, existence is inevitably shrouded. If, from this contemplation of Nature and of life, we can catch a momentary glimpse of the Ultimate Reality, that glimpse must surely reveal that Eternal Tendency towards perfection, towards righteousness, of which human life forms so fateful a part. Here, truly, we have a basis for religious life which cannot be disputed, a basis which possesses a uniting, a harmonising power which shall dissolve the dividing bonds of sect, and rebind mankind in the fellowship of a Church Universal. A religious life, which, in its application to human endeavour, means aspiration and longing for the ideal, *a striving towards something higher;* in its application to the life of the soul—retirement from the harsh clamour and materialism of the world to that inner sanctuary wherein the heart yearns for communion with the Invisible, a yearning which is part of our spiritual nature, and which, in the calmer hours of meditation, moves us to bow before the eternal mystery even as the simple, yet mysterious, life-possessing wildflower closes its petals and bends its head before the soft night-wind.

But how will this reformation—or may I not say this transformation—of religion affect the outward expression of religious life? If there is no sense of personal relationship between ourselves and the Supreme, if worship of a Personal Deity is a superstition, and prayer a futility, how shall religious life seek expression? To which it may be replied, that whereever the religious spirit exists, it will readily find channels for its manifestation. When worship is no longer a form, but a grand reality, men and women will feel all the greater need for that fellowship which is the essence of religious life, and, as a consequence, they will be naturally drawn together for the expression of mutual sympathy, for mutual communion and assistance in their strivings against evil, for the united expression of trust in, and praise of, their noblest ideal, their highest conception of the Eternal. Neither would I say that sincere prayer is futile, but, with the change in our conception of the Supreme, the spirit in which prayer is offered must undergo a corresponding change. I have already said that the offering of prayer for the satisfaction of material wants is rapidly becoming a thing of the past. There is clearly apparent in our churches a tendency towards what I may term a spirituality in prayer—that is, supplication for the satisfaction of spiritual desires rather than material needs. But it is evident that we cannot stop here. For if there is a uniformity, a reign of law, in things material, are we not justified in concluding that there is a similar uniformity or law in spiritual matters? Yet there is a clinging, and it is natural that there should be a clinging, to those modes of thought which lead to the expression of human desire for communion with higher things; and it is here that we find a rational foundation for prayer. If it is true, as I take it to be, that—

> "Prayer is the soul's sincere desire,
> Uttered or unexpressed ;
> The motion of a hidden fire
> That trembles in the breast,"

then, indeed, the custom of prayer must undergo a change, a great change for the better. We *desire* to act justly, to love mercy, to follow truth, not in the sense that these virtues may be given to us as a mother bestows gifts on a child, for this we believe to be impossible, but in the higher sense that we may have strength to overcome evil, and anger, and all unrighteousness. All sincere and true prayer is, then, aspiration, desire, "uttered or unexpressed," on bended knee, in choral chant, or in evening solitude, for communion with things divine. Prayer, aspiration, meditation, these are indissolubly interlinked and entwined in our nature, and may, indeed, be most potent when we are least conscious of their influence, more potent, perhaps, in the solitary evening walk than in the crowded house of prayer. From this meditative and prayerful attitude of mind—using the word "prayer" in the sense I have described—come that tranquillisation of the passions, that moral and spiritual benefit, that peace and calm of holiness, which are the essence of religious communion. And such prayer may be best described in the words of Coleridge:

> "Ere on my bed my limbs I lay,
> It hath not been my use to pray
> With moving lips or bended knees;
> But silently, by slow degrees,
> My spirit I to love compose,
> In humble trust mine eyelids close,
> With reverential resignation,
> No wish conceived, no thought expressed,
> Only a sense of supplication;
> A sense o'er all my soul imprest
> That I am weak, yet not unblest,
> Since in me, round me, everywhere
> Eternal strength and wisdom are."

It may be that this sense of loss of personal relationship and dependence will be still further accentuated by the change which will necessarily be made in our estimates of the character and work of Christ, and his relation to mankind. I should probably weary the attention of the reader were I to attempt to trace the influence of the reformed religion on the various doctrines of orthodox Christianity, but the doctrine of the Incarnation is of such vital importance in the orthodox scheme of salvation, that a few words on the position which Christ is likely to assume in our future thought and life may not be deemed out of place. "If Christ be not risen, then is our preaching vain, and your faith is also vain." The faith of Paul, doubtless, but not the faith of mankind. *That*, thank goodness, has its roots too deeply implanted in our common human nature to die away on the transformation of a crude doctrine into a beautiful legend. Yet Christ himself will not suffer in the change, rather will the influence of his example gain in glory and in power. Of the personalities in which the religions of mankind may be said to centre, Jesus and Sakya-Muni stand pre-eminent, and in the lives of both there are traits which bear a remarkable resemblance to each other—self-renunciation, gentleness, triumph over temptation, purification of passion, parabolical instruction—these are marked characteristics in the life of each. But as Buddha is, and perhaps always will be, looked upon as peculiarly the possession of the Eastern nations, so Christ is regarded as peculiarly the possession of the Western nations, and the story of his life will always have a distinctive value for the people of the West. The charm of that story will be all the greater to us by reason of our conviction that Jesus was a child of humanity, with some of the faults and failings common to humanity, and that his teachings, imperfect though they may be in some respects, possess, as a whole, a moral grandeur, a profoundness of insight, an exalted nobleness, which make them an ever-springing fountain of moral inspiration, an unfailing source of moral power. Divorced from the crude materialistic doctrines which theologians have imposed upon them, it is certain that the fundamental elements of Christ's teaching—and may we not say of Buddha's teaching also?—what Matthew Arnold terms the "method of inwardness" and the "secret of self-renunciation;" certain it is, I say, that these are the qualities which must reform the world, which must conquer evil, and make men and women as demi-gods. Mankind, indeed, if it has something to lose, has much to gain by a more rational, a truer estimate of the life and character of Jesus. And in this case, at any rate, the sense of loss can be only temporary. From the vulgar, materialistic fetich-worship of orthodox theology there must arise a nobler conception of Christ, a true resurrection, a resurrection of the spirit, a second Advent indeed, not with angel song and manifestation of great power and glory, but entering into our heart of hearts in the gentler guise of the mystic influence of divine example. What a dethronement of grand individuality there is in making Christ the centre of a narrow sect—a Baptist, a Trinitarian, a Christadelphian, a Plymouth Brother! What a pitiful exhibition of narrowness of mind there is in straining his sublime teachings to fit the articles of a particular church, or the trust-deeds of a little Bethel! Rescued from the contentious idolatry of a hundred petty sects, and also from the mistaken criticism of those who confound his teachings with the doctrines of orthodox Christianity, Christ will take his true place amongst the greatest of earth's heroes, and will be revered, not as a god to whom moral failure is impossible and martyrdom as naught, but as a man, who, bound and confined by all the limits and temptations which human nature imposes, yet strove against these limits and temptations with a power of self-abnegation, an intensity of passion, and a god-like courage, which flash an inspiring radiance on weary hearts through the mist and gloom of eighteen centuries. There can be no harm, indeed, in idealising Christ and Buddha, if, by so doing, we can give greater precision to our ideal of human life, and greater dignity to our conception of human nature. In freeing Christ from the blind worship of the sects, we preserve his memory from the contamination of a materialistic theology, we bring him into closer relationship with human endeavour, we are inspired with a truer and a holier reverence for the purity and sanctity of his life. For us, too, he is the Master, the acceptance of whose teachings by those who bear his name being too often, alas, but the mere repetition of vain formulas and the empty echo of his words—a cruelty more bitter than the traitor-kiss in the Garden of Gethsemane. The fuller day of Christ is not yet risen.

Such, then, are the salient points which must characterise the religious thought and life of the future. There are many other important matters upon which one might have dwelt, such matters, for example, as the interpretation and value of Scripture, and its place in the reformed religion; and no doubt hostile critics will charge me with being "discreetly silent" as to what has been termed the *sine quâ non* of religion—belief in immortality. To such objections I must plead the exigencies of space. It may be of service here, however, to ask ourselves whether such a religion as I have indicated is inconsistent with Christianity, using this term in its broadest sense. There may be some who would maintain that it would be manifestly unfair to call ourselves Christians after we have robbed the orthodox faith of most of its distinctive features; that, in rejecting such doctrines as the personality of God, the Trinity, the Incarnation, the Atonement, justification by faith, the infallibility of the Bible, eternal punishment, and many others, we are really attempting not merely to reform, but to abolish Christianity. No doubt good reasons may be advanced in favour of this contention, and it is, indeed, easy to conceive that a false compromise may be productive of harm instead of good. Timid minds, filled with apprehension at the dissolution of old beliefs, may temporarily lull themselves into a sense of security by repeating the old names and retaining the old appellations. But underneath such feelings there will often exist that vague sense of uncertainty and uneasiness which, to say the least, is not conducive to the effectiveness of religious faith, and which may result either in a shallow latitudinarianism or in a return to the old doctrines. On the other hand, however, if Christianity be looked upon as a work, a principle, rather than as a doctrine, then, surely, we may claim the title of Christian. The tendency of modern thought, even of Christian thought, is to differentiate men and women, not by petty differences about doctrine, but by the deeper principles which may be said to embody respectively the ideal, the spiritual view of life and destiny, and the materialistic, the sordid view. And if the essence of religion, of Christianity, is fellowship, why should that fellowship be denied us because of differences in doctrine? "There are diversities of operations, but it is the same God which worketh all in all." And "though I speak with the tongues of men and of angels, and have not charity, I am become as sounding brass or a tinkling cymbal." Christianity is, above all, a rule of life. It gave to the world a new commandment, a new ideal. That commandment, that ideal—though the one has been disobeyed and the other dimmed by those who have borne the Christian name—that commandment and that ideal, I say, have been the real basis of the historical continuity of the Christian Church. And in striving to make that basis firmer and surer, we are in reality striving to strengthen the continuity of the Church, and to render its work more effective. In this sense, then, our work may be termed Christian work. Names, however, are, after all, of little moment, so long as the reality is there. Our opponents may think to discredit us by labelling us with opprobrious epithets, and yet, if we felt inclined to make use of the same weapons, we might retort upon them with the words of him, who, being asked at his martyrdom to renounce his heresies and so regain his freedom, waved his hand towards his persecutors with the cry: "Away with the Atheists."

To the great bulk of mankind the natural progression of life, of thought, seems to bring no pain. Progress, advance, is almost unconscious. Old doctrines die away with the old generation, and the new generation easily accustoms itself to the new thoughts, the new teachings, which have insensibly usurped the place of the old. Perhaps it is only to the few that the change from the old faith to the new brings the swelling surgings and re-surgings of the mind, and the bitterness of inward strife. To some, the prospect of release from the bondage of false and gloomy doctrines may come with all the joyousness of new-found freedom; to others, the natural conservatism of the mind will make the inward struggle sadder and more prolonged. There will be a longing for the old faith, for the consolations which, ofttimes before, gave calm to the mind and solace to the soul, but which, in the light of fuller knowledge, are seen to be illusory and unsatisfying. The feelings and habits of thought which have been woven into the minds of unnumbered generations are exceedingly tenacious of life and difficult to cast aside. It is, indeed, useless to pretend that there is no pain attendant on the dispelling of illusions, on the weakening of faith in things once thought to be true and holy. To some natures such pain is the penalty of mental and moral progress. It is a feature, more or less marked, of every age, of every change in religious thought—yea, it has been a distinguishing feature of the evolution of Christianity itself. And it is not only by those who have once experienced the consolations of the Christian faith that this painful sense of loss is felt. It is felt, though perhaps not in an equal degree, even unto the second and third generation. I may say (if the reader will pardon a personal reference for the purpose of illustrating my contention) that the present writer, though brought up from birth in an atmosphere of extreme sceptical thought absolutely devoid of spiritual aspiration, and in which scorn and contempt for the Christian faith were marked elements, has often felt himself swayed as by some powerful hidden impulse towards the faith of his ancestors, the unconscious assumptions, feelings, and habits of thought of preceding generations welling up in his mind and producing a solitary yearning of the heart for a something which it feels it cannot possess. Habits of thought, like habits of body, are hereditary, and the breaking of such habits necessarily produces painful consequences. Yet—

> "I hold it truth, with him who sings
> To one clear harp in divers tones,
> That men may rise on stepping-stones
> Of their dead selves to higher things."

So that when we are asked, "Why, if this loss of faith is productive of sorrow and pain, do you assert that the newer faith is of a nobler type?" we reply, first, because at whatever cost, at whatever sacrifice of happiness, the valiant, the religious mind must ever be content to follow "the high, white star of truth;" and, second, because wherever faith in good continues after faith in happiness, temporal or eternal, as a *necessary result* of that good, has departed, such faith must surely be of the noblest type. The greater the difficulty in the way of goodness, the more obstacles there are to be overcome, the nobler will be the victory, and it is always to the highest nobleness that the human mind aspires. It is for this reason that we believe the new faith is so much superior to the old, and that its breadth, its grandeur, its intellectual and moral beauty will more than compensate for the loss of the old. So that those who, in moments of retrospection, look back longingly to the faith of their childhood, will find solace in the reflection that a change of faith does not mean a decay, but rather a growth, a development of faith. They will find that theological doctrines and barren formulas are inadequate to gratify man's spiritual cravings, to satisfy the hunger of the soul. These doctrines have served their purpose, and in their place there must come a higher religion, a truer spiritual life, a living faith, having the power to quicken the soul of man, to impregnate it with loftier aspirations, to prepare it for vaster issues;—a religion which will render unbelief an absurdity, and infidelity—unfaithfulness to what is good—a crime;—a religion which needs no name, but whose watchword is "Duty." And so long as the thing is there, the shibboleth will take care of itself. Intolerant religious classification will cease with the decadence of theology.

To the orthodox Christian, who regards his own little Bethel as the true resting-place and his own doctrine as the only means of salvation, it may seem strange that I should close this essay by quoting the words of Christ in justification of my views; he may, indeed, feel tempted to exclaim: "What right have *you* to quote the words of the Master?" But, as I have already said, Jesus belongs to humanity, not to a sect, and the time is rapidly drawing nigh when his teaching will be accepted in its higher and truer meaning, so that we can to-day repeat his words with a firmer conviction of their certain realisation: "The hour cometh, when ye shall neither in this mountain, nor yet at Jerusalem, worship the Father. But the hour cometh, and now is, when the true worshippers shall worship the Father in spirit and in truth."[1] This may be said to be a statement of religion in its inward or subjective aspect; and for a statement of religion in its outward or objective aspect I may cite that fine allegory, in which, at the most solemn moment of the soul's existence—a circumstance which gives the passage greater weight and authority—the touchstone is applied to the religious life of each individual soul, and the touchstone is not doctrine, nor faith, but conduct. "I was an hungered, and ye gave me meat; I was thirsty, and ye gave me drink; I was a stranger, and ye took me in; naked, and ye clothed me; I was sick, and ye visited me; I was in prison, and ye came unto me. Then shall the righteous answer Him, saying, Lord, when saw we thee an hungered, and fed thee? or thirsty, and gave thee drink? When saw we thee a stranger, and took thee in? or naked, and clothed thee? Or when saw we thee sick, or in prison, and came unto thee? And the King shall answer and say unto them, Verily I say unto you, inasmuch as ye have done it unto one of the least of these my brethren, ye have done it unto me."

Here, then, we have a statement of religion to which,

---

[1] John iv. 21, 23. Verse 22 is obviously an interpolation.

in its widest interpretation—and who would dare to give it a narrow interpretation?—none can take exception. Ever feeling that—

> "The awful shadow of some unseen Power
> Floats, though unseen, among us,"

an invisible Power which makes for perfection; we also feel that we can best place ourselves in harmony with the workings of this Power by being true to the best we know or can conceive. Hence, it is not in the narrow bonds of dogma, not in the restricted spirit of doctrinal codes and trust-deeds, but wherever the heart of man shall beat to high resolve, wherever the human mind aspires to commune with things divine, there shall man worship "in spirit and in truth."

There is a silent solitary temple of the heart wherein each man may worship. It may be with the babbling of empty echoes, and the chaunting of lifeless words, or it may be with the glow and enthusiasm of a heavenly fire, which flashes its radiance on surrounding life as the stars flash their myriad beams of light on the gloom and darkness of the night. It is for us, the eternal children of Humanity, to aid in the consummation of this worship, knowing that the fruition of our righteous service shall never pass into nothingness, but shall rather be as a divine spiritual sustenance—a perennial source of strength to the soul, exercising an everlasting influence on the sons of men.

CHAPTER III.

THE SANCTIONS OF MORALITY IN THEIR RELATION TO RELIGIOUS LIFE.

ONE of the most hopeful of the signs which are now manifesting themselves amid the doubts and questionings which characterise the moral and religious life of the latter half of the nineteenth century, is the intense purpose with which the moral spirit—the power of conscience—is animating human endeavour. We see it on every hand—in literature, in politics, in every movement of social reform. Human relationships are unconsciously being readjusted and regulated in accordance with those higher ideals which are slowly taking possession of the human mind. Even our industrial and business life is being influenced, and may ultimately be permeated, by the new moral spirit. "Conscience," says Professor Clifford, "springs out of the habit of judging things from the point of view of all, and not of one." It is this habit which, notwithstanding the break-up of old faiths and beliefs, is daily becoming of stronger force in the moral life of humanity. And perplexing as the fact may be to the orthodox believer, a moment's consideration will show that it is a necessary result of the changed conditions of human thought. Rebellion against traditional authority in matters of faith and belief must of necessity create the need for the establishment of superior standards; and thus man is thrown back upon his own intellectual and spiritual resources. The "continuous adjustment of internal to external relations" is a condition of the moral and intellectual, no less than of the physical life. Hence we see that at the period of the Reformation the revolt of Wyclif, Luther, Calvin, and their coadjutors, produced an intellectual and moral awakening which, casting aside the authoritative and traditional interpretation of the inspired records, felt itself bound, if the religious life was to continue, to provide new interpretations, new doctrines, new modes of faith, new sanctions of morality. Hence, again, in our own day, through the active or tacit rejection of the received interpretation, men are driven to find a surer basis for religious faith, a higher sanction for moral endeavour. That the search will ultimately prove successful no one can doubt who has faith in the potentialities of human nature. The passage through the negative and positive stages of the struggle may be long and wearisome, but we have not only Time on our side, we have the primordial instincts of our being.

The negative phase of that struggle against traditional authority may, roughly speaking, be divided into two aspects—the historical and the moral. With the historical aspect it is not the intention of this essay to deal. That a large proportion of thinking people view the question from the historical standpoint, and are ready to stake their sincerest and most hallowed beliefs on the worth of the historical evidence to be adduced in their favour, is, of course, beyond question. But it is obvious that from the very nature of the case the worth of the historical evidence is purely a matter of opinion. Even if Christ were to descend among us to-day and show us the nail-marks in his hands and feet, and the spear-wound in his side, there would still be more than one doubting Thomas who would demand a certificate of birth and parentage. But when the events to be investigated are removed eighteen centuries from our own time, to an age in which the condition of knowledge and of the human mind predisposed men to accept the miraculous without question, when the methods of reporting and sifting evidence were necessarily of a very simple and primitive nature, and gave unlimited scope for the introduction of forged documents, and the consequent accretion of legend, then the difficulties are immensely increased even for well-informed men. And as for the masses—or those of them who take an interest in the subject—they see that to attempt to arrive at an impartial estimate of the evidence is, for them, hopeless; they simply ignore the historical aspect of the question, and, judging from the moral standpoint, make their own moral sense the criterion of the supposed supernatural. Those, however, who would have us believe that morality is based upon a revealed system of religion will at once say that it is presumptuous on the part of man to measure the supernatural by his own petty standard of right and wrong. But that is exactly what the supernaturalist himself does when he interprets Scripture according to his own theological notions. We all know how entirely belief depends upon interpretation, and how interpretation depends upon knowledge. "No man," says Matthew Arnold, "no man, who knows nothing else, knows even his Bible." Because, of course, our interpretation of the Bible depends upon our knowledge of human nature, of history, and of the religions of the world. In like manner, our conceptions of morality, even though based upon what we suppose to be revealed truth, are modified by education, custom, and environment. Thus the so-called infallible guide, through the very process of conception by conditioned and fallible media, takes upon itself the human qualities—prejudice, passion, inclinations, desires—which render its supposed infallibility worthless. Gods alone can understand and appreciate gods.

The supernaturalist may further object that to judge the supernatural by the fallible moral sense of man is to dwarf religion into mere morality. In this he is wrong. For it is not solely in the promptings of the moral sense that man finds religion, it is in the yearning of the individual soul for communion with the Supreme. The mere procession of the sun and stars, of the seasons, of day and night, and the consciousness, in man, of the self and not-self, which implies a still more complete consciousness, i.e., of the unity which includes both—these, I say, are sufficient to imbue the mind with the sense of a Presence which transcends the individual and the finite. Hence, religion is not merely "morality touched with emotion," it is something more than this. The definition is hardly comprehensive enough, for though "morality touched with emotion" *is* religion—religion on its practical side, the outward embodiment of an inward faith—yet in religious feeling, there is something besides this, something which it is difficult to define: that upward striving or aspiration of the soul which the Eastern sages would have named a yearning after the Beyond—an inward, spontaneous emotion which shrinks from contact with the outer world, and which belongs to the meditative life rather than to the life of action.

But for moral guidance man is thrown back upon himself. No voice issues from the darkness; the sun and stars are as silent as the night, and the light which is to illumine our path must be kindled, though with unspeakable anguish, in our own hearts. "A good man out of the good treasure of his heart bringeth forth that which is good; and an evil man out of the evil treasure of his heart bringeth forth that which is evil; for out of the abundance of the heart the mouth speaketh." And as in the moral, so in the intellectual life. The ignorant will find Shakespeare dry, tedious, and uninteresting; the bigot will see in the Bible the reflection of his own distorted and narrow views; but the wise will find in both, not the light itself, but the oil with which to feed the lamp of knowledge. We may, indeed, assimilate experience, knowledge, and wisdom, but these can be turned to practical service only in so far as we can use them as weapons in the perpetual combat which wages in our own souls. We may pass through periods of intense mental suffering, of remorse, of the agony of shame, but what shall the suffering avail, if, through the hardening of conscience, it brings no loftier purpose, no gentler spirit, no purer life? No, it is within ourselves redemption must be wrought, and the deeper we fathom the mysterious problems of our own hearts, the clearer will be our vision of the possibilities of human endeavour.

But those who are unwilling to accept any statement of natural religion in contradistinction to what is termed revealed religion, and who look with apprehension upon all attempts to weaken the orthodox faith, will view with equal dismay any attempt to build up a natural, as distinguished from a supernatural, ethical system. If it can be shown, however, that the fundamental doctrines of the supposed supernatural system are inadequate to meet the demands of the higher life, and that, by this system, morality is set upon a false foundation, a foundation which, being open to question, weakens the very springs of morality, then the way will be cleared for an impartial examination of that system which makes no pretensions to having received the impress of divine authority, but which, making moral truth self-evident, or at least verifiable by human experience, sets morality on a basis which is unaffected by the shiftings of theological doctrine.

First, then, let us briefly examine the fundamental principle on which the supernatural system bases itself—the principle that morality depends on belief in certain theological doctrines—*e.g.*, that God is a Person who thinks and loves, and that the revelation of His will in inspired writings, or in conscience, is the ultimate standard of right and wrong. We need not here dwell on the doctrines themselves, but simply on the statement that belief in them is necessary to the establishment of a true system of morality. "Conduct," says the orthodox theologian, "being the outcome of belief, where belief is right, conduct also will be right—where there is faith in what is good, right works will naturally follow." Hence "we are accounted righteous before God by Faith, not for our own works or deservings." It is at once obvious that the whole controversy depends entirely on the significance we attach to the word "belief." No one would deny that belief moulds conduct, that faith in what is good is the inspirer of right action. But not even the most violent theological partisan would venture to say, for example, that goodness is dependent on a belief in the Trinity, as opposed to a belief in the Unity, of God, or that integrity and uprightness are the exclusive possession of those who accept as true certain incredible narratives in the Old Testament. The fact is, there is something contradictory in our ideas respecting the influence of belief on conduct. On the one hand, we see men of various creeds living useful, honest, truthful and even noble lives—a fact which seems to point to the conclusion that theological belief has not necessarily any influence on conduct; on the other hand, we are bound to believe that wherever error prevails, such error must have its due effect in preventing the mind from seeing and accepting the truth, and so must, in the long run, have a mischievous influence on human conduct and human life. Let us, then, try to obtain a clear understanding as to

E

what we mean when we speak of belief influencing conduct. As to the importance of having right beliefs we are all agreed. We regard it as the most sacred duty of the parent to implant in the mind of the child those affections and antipathies which predispose it to choose the good and reject the evil. We inculcate the virtue of obedience, teaching the child to believe that the rule of father or mother is a far better guide than its own selfish inclinations and desires, so that, by the time it reaches maturity, long years of discipline may have firmly implanted in its mind the belief—the *religious* belief, I may say—that right conduct must be founded on some higher law than the promptings of self-will. In like manner, Plato urges that it is the duty of the State to give a true education to its youth, "because he who has received this true education of the inner being will most shrewdly perceive omissions or faults in Art and Nature, and with a true taste, while he praises and rejoices over and receives into his soul the good, and becomes noble and good, he will justly blame and hate the bad, now in the days of his youth, even before he is able to know the reason why; and when Reason comes he will recognise and salute her as a friend with whom his education has made him long familiar."[1] Thus we see that belief lies at the very foundation of conduct. How, then, are we to account for the fact that men of the most antagonistic beliefs live virtuous and even noble lives? The difficulty can hardly be solved by dividing belief into speculative and practical, for some of our most cherished be-

---

[1] *The Republic*, Book iii. 402. Jowett's translation.

liefs, even those which are the foundation of conduct, are speculative. What, for example, can be more speculative than the question—What is justice? Perhaps the solution of the difficulty will be found in this—that religious beliefs involve a certain conception or theory of life; these ideal conceptions embody themselves in a framework of doctrine; from these doctrines certain rules and principles are deduced, and these rules and principles are applied (1) to the conduct of the individual in the ordinary affairs of everyday life; and (2) to the conduct of the individual in relation to society and to the State. There is thus a gulf between our ideal conceptions or religious beliefs and the application of the principles deduced from these conceptions or beliefs, and it is in the bridging of this gulf, or in the transition from ideal conceptions to the deduction and application of principles, that we discern the issue of similar types of conduct from apparently antagonistic beliefs and doctrines. The man who believes in the existence of a personal Deity, or Will, as the absolute right, will deduce from that, through a body of doctrine, that each individual should strive to place himself in harmony with that Will by the rightness of his life; the man who rejects such a belief, and substitutes for it a conception of the Supreme as "the eternal power, not ourselves, which makes for righteousness," will deduce from that that it is the duty of each individual to place himself in harmony with the "stream of tendency by which all things seek to fulfil the law of their being." That is, each individual mind, in so far as it possesses any religious belief worth the name, defines its conceptions and ideals in terms of its own, and educes its principles according to its own constitution, temperament, and habits of thought. When, then, Protestant theologians tell us that "we are accounted righteous before God by faith and not for our own works or deservings," or that belief—meaning, of course, belief in certain theological doctrines—is necessary to salvation, we see at once the mistake into which they fall. They attempt the impossible task of "fitting on" to each individual mind the conceptions and ideals which are adapted only to a certain order of mind. Behind, or inseparably connected with belief, is character, and the threads of character and belief are so inextricably intertwined that it is impossible to lay them bare, and determine the extent or the intensity of the influence of each upon the other. An unsympathetic, narrow-minded, bigoted man will have corresponding beliefs; a sympathetic, large-minded, tolerant man will have converse beliefs. Hence, belief being adapted to the character and capacity of each individual mind, it must take manifold and diverse shapes. To the adherent of the Salvation Army the principles of the Synthetic Philosophy are as a sealed book; to the Fijian the theological doctrines of orthodox Christianity are equally incomprehensible. And not only does belief differ with difference in character and mental capacity, it varies in degree or intensity with increase of knowledge and change of environment. New discoveries in science and history, new methods of criticism, new worlds of facts, shake it to its foundations, and necessitate a readjustment of the old habits of thought to the knowledge assimilated by an ever-widening experience. If, then, character and belief act and react upon each other, and if, as a natural consequence, *all* beliefs influence conduct either for good or for evil, shall we formulate our creed and say—*This* only is the true belief, and in this only will mankind find redemption! In that we should merely be imitating our orthodox friends, who, to use Carlyle's phrase, would fit their "poor wigs and Church tippets" to every order of mind. No, the only thing we can assert with certainty is, that in so far as belief is the outcome of a sincere and earnest endeavour to reach the truth, a sacred conviction by which a man determines his life's conduct, in so far is it an influence for good. But where belief is merely the result of custom or convention, a profession of faith having no root in the inner life of man, a formula which nurses the mind into an unreflecting credulity regarding its relations to the Unseen, then it may be said to have an influence for evil. And even in this case, how much of the evil shall we say is due to character and how much to belief? In the ultimate resort, then, we are forced to the conclusion that the moral progress of the individual depends, not on the adoption of any special theological or metaphysical belief, but on that natural expansion and development of the faculties which, gradually freeing the mind from error, gives clearer vision and deeper insight into the difficulties which burden our human life. That is, that in the presence of the infinite Unknown, error is a necessary stage in the progress of the mind, and false beliefs perish only with the growth of knowledge. And further, that both character and belief must be tested not by *à priori* notions as to the constitution and regulation of the universe, but by their results in conduct, as, indeed, they are so tested by Christ in his allegory of the last judgment: "Inasmuch as ye have done it unto one of the least of these my brethren, ye have done it unto Me."

I do not, however, put forward this theory as in any sense an adequate solution of the problems connected with belief, but rather for the purpose of suggesting to the mind of the reader a train of thought which may help towards a solution. The principles, causes, desires, motives, which impel man to action, influencing him unconsciously, pushing him, as it were, with unseen hands, restraining him by phantom fears implanted in his nature by the ignorance and superstition of those who have gone before—all these are so profoundly hidden from our gaze that we can but dimly conjecture as to the foundations of belief. The Catholic, the Protestant, the Agnostic, may all be men of high moral character, but if one only of the doctrines they represent be true, the others must be false, and, where the wrong is advocated, the pernicious effect must make itself felt either in the life or the teachings of those who are influenced by the wrong doctrine. We may, indeed, take the ground that each doctrine is right in its place and for the order of mind which accepts it, each mind being so constituted as to be capable of receiving only certain forms of belief, but in this we should be getting perilously near the absurd optimistic doctrine that "Whatever is, is right," and ignoring the very obvious effect which environment has upon belief and character. Where education or environment is wrong, it must produce an imperfect type of human character; where environment is right, it must tend to produce a perfect type.

Difficult, then, though it may be to determine the extent of the influence of character on belief, of belief on character, and of both on conduct, the fact that that influence exists must be regarded as unquestionable. Mr. Arnold tells us that conduct "is a very simple thing," and that "all moralists are agreed as to its simplicity."[1] Of that, however, we are not quite so sure. True, conduct is simple enough in so far as it concerns matters of ordinary individual life—we know, for example, that it is wrong to lie or to steal. But it is not so simple when we come to consider the relations of the individual to society or to the State. Here we are at once brought face to face with the problems suggested by the words "rights" and "duties." And the solution of these problems involves matters not merely of a speculative nature, but matters which affect social life and conduct at a hundred points. As to this no one can be more explicit than John Stuart Mill. "It is hardly possible," he says, "to exaggerate the mischief of a false philosophy. The notion that truths external to the mind may be known by intuition or consciousness, independently of observation and experience, is, I am persuaded, in these times the great intellectual support of false doctrines and bad institutions."[2]

[1] *Literature and Dogma*, chap i. sec. i.
[2] *Autobiography*, p. 225.

The difference between the two schools of philosophy—that of Intuition and that of Experience and Association—"is not a mere matter of abstract speculation; it is full of practical consequences, and lies at the foundation of all the greatest differences of practical opinion in an age of progress."[1] This, then—the influence of speculative belief on conduct—may be regarded as an indisputable fact. And now let us note the use which the theologian makes of it. "Conduct," he says, "being influenced by belief, as man is responsible for his conduct, he must also be responsible for the belief which influences conduct." But here we must be on our guard. We see at once that there must be some flaw in the deduction when we ask, "What! Is man responsible for not believing in the doctrine of the Trinity, the inspiration and infallibility of Scripture, or the Personality of God?" And yet, this is what the orthodox theologian would have us infer. True, it is not often nowadays that the doctrine of the culpability of moral error is so nakedly stated as in the following passage from Dr. Whewell's *Elements of Morality :* "We do not excuse the moderns who, now that there has taken place this great revelation, elevating the moral views and spiritual hopes of man, refuse to believe the truths thus established. They who do this reject the light which has come into the world, and the blindness in which they remain is not only their misfortune, but their fault." And again: "A person to whom the truths brought to light by the Christian revelation have been fully presented, and who dis-

[1] *Ibid.* p. 273.

believes them, is as blameable or as unhappy as a man would be who should deny the government of Providence, the reality of morality, the necessity of repentance in transgressors, and of moral progress in all men."[1] Possibly, however, Dr. Whewell's theology is now generally regarded as somewhat antiquated. But the same position is still held by orthodox theologians, though it is defended in language which is a little more respectful. Mr. Gladstone, for example, maintaining the same doctrine, illustrates his argument thus: "A large part of the world have held that the root of civil power is not in the community but in its head. In opposition to this doctrine, the American written Constitution and the entire American tradition teach the right of a nation to self-government. And these propositions, which have divided, and still divide, the world, open out respectively into vast systems of irreconcilable ideas and laws, practices, and habits of mind. Will any rational man contend that these conflicting systems have been adopted, upheld, and enforced on one side and the other in the daylight of pure reasoning only, and that moral or immoral causes have had nothing to do with their adoption? That the intellect has worked impartially, like a steam-engine, and that selfishness, love of fame, love of money, love of power, envy, wrath, and malice, or again, bias in its least noxious form, have never had anything to do with generating the opposing movements, or the frightful collisions in which they have resulted? If we say that they have not, we contradict the universal judgment of man-

[1] Book iii., chap. xii.

kind. If we say they have, then mental processes are not automatic, but may be influenced by the will, and by the passions, affections, habits, fancies, that sway the will."[1] Therefore, argues Mr. Gladstone, as will influences belief, volition being a subject of moral judgment, man is responsible for his beliefs. But the sophistry is at once apparent. Mr. Gladstone confuses feeling and volition, links character—" passions, affections, habits, and fancies "—with will, quietly assumes the identity of the two, and then proceeds to draw the inference which he desires—that speculative beliefs are influenced by the will, and that, therefore, man is responsible for his beliefs. It is a mere truism, however, that there are elements in character for which the individual is not responsible. Every man, Mr. Gladstone himself, is influenced by passions, prejudices, affections, early training hereditary predisposition, but he would never assert that man is responsible for the predispositions which are stamped upon his mental organisation before birth, or for the prejudices and affections which are given by early training, yet these are vital elements of character. Imitating Mr. Gladstone's method of reasoning, we might say that there are certain elements of character—hereditary predisposition, and the prejudices and affections given by early training—for which the individual is not responsible, that these elements of character have a decided influence on belief, that, therefore, man is not responsible for his beliefs. And this is, indeed, true in so far as belief is influenced by elements in character for which we are

[1] *North American Review*, May, 1888.

not responsible. But this is only half the truth. We know that there are elements in character, for which man is responsible,[1] habits and prejudices which are the result of mental indolence, petulance and passion which are the freaks of an unguarded temper; and in so far as belief is influenced by these, man may be said to be responsible to some extent for his beliefs, or perhaps it would be better to say, for the *formation* of his beliefs, just as we say that we are not responsible for evil thoughts, because thoughts come naturally and unbidden, but that we are responsible for the *retention* of such thoughts in our mind when we know their evil character. The mistake of the theologian consists in grouping together both the responsible and the non-responsible elements of character, and in subordinating these to the will. Having thus made will supreme over both feeling and thought, he draws the sweeping inference that, volition being the subject of moral judgments, man is responsible for his beliefs, or, in other words, that man is responsible for not believing in the doctrine of the Trinity, the divinity of Christ, the infallibility of Scripture, or the Personality of God. Hence, it is necessary to discriminate, so far as we can, between those elements of character for which we may be said to be responsible, and those for which we are not, and the more we attempt to discriminate, the more clearly shall we become aware of the impossibility of delivering judgment as to moral responsi-

---

[1] I assume, for the moment, the freedom of the will, which, in its relation to moral responsibility, will be discussed in another chapter.

bility in any particular case of belief, or of arriving at anything like a clear and definite rule or law in the matter, not merely because there are innate differences in the constitution of every individual mind, but because, as before observed, the threads of character and the threads of belief are so inextricably interwoven that it is impossible to disentangle them, and follow each to its natural end in conduct. Even where sincere and earnest belief brings evil results, though we condemn the belief, we do not judge the believer. This is, of course, merely a restatement of the truth that man must have knowledge ere he can be deemed responsible. Error in the formation of opinion may be said to arise from ignorance, and we may conclude with Plato, that " no soul is voluntarily ignorant of anything. And what is ignorance but the aberration of a mind which is bent on truth, and in which the process of understanding is perverted?"[1]

We find, then, that the orthodox theory respecting the culpability of error in belief runs counter to our moral sense. And not only this, we find that belief itself—in the concrete form of doctrine—is no guarantee of moral conduct, but that the impellents to moral action lie, as it were, behind belief, in the very texture of our moral character. Where, then, shall we look for the sanctions of morality, for incentives to moral endeavour, or deterrents from wrong-doing? Perhaps it would be too much to say that the orthodox theory of rewards and punishments has died a natural death. True, we have travelled a long way since Paley declared virtue to be " the doing good to

[1] *Sophist*, 228. Jowett's translation.

mankind in obedience to the will of God, and for the sake of everlasting happiness." Nevertheless, what is termed the "selfish system" is still occasionally advocated in all its nakedness. M. de Laveleye, for example, declares that "a denial of the spirituality of the soul uproots all reasonable motives for being just and honest;" and he even goes so far as to ask—"If I can enrich myself and escape the penal code, why should I not do so?"[1] Nor is this teaching confined solely to orthodox circles—we find it expounded in a modified form even by rational religionists. Dr. Martineau, for example, has laid it down that if there is no supernatural authority of which the moral law is the expression, "nothing remains but to pronounce the sense of responsibility a mere illusion; the fiduciary aspect of life must disappear: there is no trust committed to us, no eye to watch, no account to render; we have but to settle terms with our neighbours and all is well. Purity within, faithfulness when alone, harmony and depth in the secret affections, are guarded by no cautionary presence and aided by no sacred sympathy; it may be happy for us if we keep them, but if we mar them it is our own affair, and there is none to reproach us or put us to shame."[2] The consideration of such a position need not detain us. That cannot be considered virtue which slips its moral moorings the moment the All-seeing eye is withdrawn, or which refrains from immoral actions only through fear of the penal code; it is merely another form of that calculating prudence which is to

[1] *Contemporary Review*, July, 1888.
[2] *A Study of Religion.* Vol. ii. p. 40.

be met with every day amongst men of business. However necessary the "fear o' hell" may have been in the past for the purpose of keeping wretches in order, it cannot be pretended that such a doctrine is consonant with the highest standard of ethics. The man who refrains from evil-doing solely through fear of punishment may be regarded with the same sentiments as those with which we look upon a child who obeys its parents only through perpetual fear of the rod. As Mr. Ruskin, in his characteristic way, observes: "When men have got to the point of believing virtue impossible but through dread of hell, they have got *into* it." For the highest examples of heroism we look to those who perform perilous service from purely disinterested motives, to those who labour silently and unknown in obedience to the call of duty, believing that their meed of service will bear fruit in the ultimate triumph of good. So long as human relationships exist, the sense of responsibility can never be "a mere illusion." Though there be no eye to watch, the account must be rendered in its strictest integrity, and the trust committed to our charge is the more sacred in that its violation, either in relation to our fellows or to our highest self, though atoned for, may never be repaired.

Of late years there has been manifested a desire to lay greater stress on conformity to what is termed the "Will of God," or the Moral Law, as the rule of conduct, independently either of hope of reward or fear of punishment. But here, again, arises the difficulty as to interpretation. For what is the Moral Law? Dr. Martineau speaks of it as "a law which holds for all thinking and voluntary beings." Why, then, do the most conscientious men lay down antagonistic principles for the guidance of conduct? The phrase is often carelessly used as though it had a definite and well-understood meaning—an oracular command embodying Supreme Wisdom. But that which presents itself with all the force and solemnity of eternal equity or moral law to one man, may appear a very immoral law to another.[1] The same difficulty occurs with the phrase "Will of God." We are all willing to admit that conduct should aid in the "eternal tendency" which makes for righteousness or perfection, and if we are content with this as the expression of the will of God, then nothing further need be said on this point. But we know that the phrase, as used by orthodox theologians, means much more than this. It is used to denote something apart from, or above, the ordinary course of Nature, some supposed special revelation made to man by an all-wise and omnipotent personal Deity. But, as already observed, even if we assume the truth of the doctrine of special revelation, we are met, on the very threshold of our inquiry, by the finite nature of man's faculties, involving, of necessity, a continual change and modification of the interpretation of the inspired records, and a consequent change

[1] Take, for example, the question of boycotting, which, I believe, is likely to assume great, and perhaps terrible, importance during the course of the next generation. We know that some regard the practice as decidedly immoral, and urge that it should be put down by force of law, and yet the rack-rented farmer or the "new unionist" may look upon it as the first of duties to treat the rack-renter, or the tyrannical employer of labour, as a moral leper.

in religion and morals. If, in the revelation, certain passages which require the performance of stated acts, or obedience to certain commands, are regarded in one age as strictly literal, and in another age as purely figurative, the important bearing such a difference in interpretation must have on morals is obvious. Numerous examples might be given, but I need name only one, that is, the change which has come over the Christian world as to the application of those texts which inculcate the persecution of heretics. We all know—or perhaps I should say that all ought to know—what bloodshed and suffering these teachings have caused. Happily, a change has come over mankind. The texts are still there, but they are either differently interpreted or are discreetly allowed to drop out of remembrance. If, then, interpretation is subject to frequent and radical change, we are forced to the conclusion that, *to man*, the conception of the will of God is also subject to change; and thus, that which is supposed to be an infallible guide to conduct is found to vary with the mental characteristics of each individual—the "Will of God" *for man*, is what man conceives it to be. The theologian may point to Christ as the "perfect example," but when, as we see, the life and teachings of Christ are susceptible of such wide difference in interpretation, the "perfect example" becomes to us simply a portion of that universal experience from which we deduce our systems of morality. The argument seems conclusive. Once admit the right of private interpretation of Scripture, and no limits can be set to that right. The Protestant theologian is logically forced, in the last resort, into the position of the evolutionist, who regards man's knowledge of that which constitutes the moral law as ever growing wider and fuller by reason of accumulating experience.

It may be of service to note one other position which orthodox theologians assume respecting the relation of moral endeavour to supernatural sanctions. It is said that God has endowed man with conscience, thereby giving him the means by which he may interpret the Supreme Will. Behind this statement there is, of course, the assumption that God is a moral and intelligent *Person*, and that the endowment of His creatures with what we term conscience is part of that "divine plan" of the universe which is peculiar to orthodox theology. All this, as Matthew Arnold would say, is "in the air." That man has a conscience we know ; that this conscience has been evolved according to the natural tendency of things towards human perfectibility, this we also know. Here we are on safe ground; more than this we do not feel justified in asserting. Those who, like Dr. Martineau, insist that conscience is an endowment from a supernatural authority, that it is the "delegate of a Sovereign Righteousness," have to deal with the very obvious fact that it often fails to determine what is right and what is wrong. Sometimes its verdicts conflict with the almost universal standard of justice. Good and conscientious intentions pave the way to hell. We all know that some of the most merciless inquisitors of the Catholic Church were men of unblemished integrity, whose motives were unquestionable, whose conscientiousness none could doubt.

F

Further illustration is needless, however. I merely wish to point out to the reader the unavoidable inference from the position of the theologians, an inference which is repugnant to the moral sense of man, and which, to-day, is leading many minds to reject orthodox Christianity—namely, that the moral and intelligent Governor of the universe has endowed man with an imperfect faculty for the determination of what is right and what is wrong, yet will, according to the "plan," condemn conscientious wrong-doers and wrong-believers to punishment, or, at least, will deprive them of that happiness which will be bestowed on others, even though they have followed the promptings of that very faculty with which He has endowed them. If this inference be not allowed, then we are forced to the conclusion that conscientious atheists will inhabit the Kingdom of Heaven.

To return from this digression. Apart from the foregoing considerations, it is evident that the so-called Will of God, in the theological sense of that term, has little or nothing to do with the performance of our moral duties. Men act honestly and uprightly, are charitable and kind to their less favoured fellow-men, not merely because these actions are in conformity with the supposed Will of God, but because they feel that such acts are inherently right, and are part of what George Eliot calls "the divine power against evil, widening the skirts of light, and making the struggle against darkness narrower." This, indeed, is the only sense in which we can speak, with any degree of certainty, of the Will of the Supreme and its relation to mankind. The position here taken that the Will of God, in its theological signification, has nothing to do with the performance of right actions, has been so well stated by Sir Thomas Browne in his *Lectures on Ethics*, that I will conclude this portion of my subject by quoting his words: "The mother, though she should at the moment forget altogether that there is a God in Nature, would still turn with moral horror from the thought of murdering the little prattler who is sporting at her knee, and who is not more beautiful to her eye by external charms and graces than beautiful to her heart by the thousand tendernesses which every day and almost every hour is developing; while the child, who perhaps has scarcely heard that there is a God, or who at least is ignorant of any Will of God, in conformity with which virtue consists, is still in his very ignorance developing those moral feelings which are supposed to be inconsistent with such ignorance, and would not have the same feeling of complacency in repaying the parental caresses with acts of intentional injury as when he repays them with expressions of reciprocal love. Of all the mothers who, at this moment, on the earth, are exercised, and virtuously exercised, in maternal duties around the cradles of their infants, there is perhaps not one who is thinking that God has commanded her to love her offspring, and to perform for them the many offices of love that are necessary for preserving the lives which are so dear to her."

We see, then, that the supposed supernatural sanctions of morality, whatever part they may have played in the development of man's moral nature, are merely the phantoms of man's imagination, changing as human nature changes, here taking the aspect of terrible cruelty, there the seductive charm of voluptuous ease, here, again, the refined pleasure of a hypothetical heaven. All are based upon a false foundation. Dispel the phantoms—the fear of punishment, the desire for voluptuous ease, the hope of future pleasure—and, on the hypothesis, morality is doomed. But this we cannot believe. And so upon us lies the responsibility of showing a truer and surer basis for moral endeavour. The old creeds are crumbling, and yet never was there a time when clearer light and surer guidance were needed. All our problems—economic, political, social—resolve themselves ultimately into the moral and religious problem. And though our old beliefs have proved to be but the baseless fabric of a vision, and now, when help is needed, they give us none, of this, at any rate, we may be sure, that so long as there arises the cry of human sorrow or the need of human sympathy, morality, founded on an impregnable basis, shall withstand the shocks of time and circumstance, and slowly but surely rise above the shifting impulses of changing and decaying creeds.

CHAPTER IV.

THE SANCTIONS OF MORALITY.

OUR previous examination of the more important features of the ethics of supernaturalism will now assist us in shadowing forth the development of what may be termed humanitarian ethics, for it is to development, and to the laws which condition development, that we must look for guidance in the matter. Morality is essentially progressive. The ideals of one age become transformed into the practical realities of succeeding ages. The movement of ethical theories is alternately from Individualism to Socialism, and back from Socialism to Individualism. I use these terms, of course, in their ethical rather than in their political significance; that is, "Socialism" as implying a moral unity or order which requires the submission of the individual to its authority; and "Individualism," as implying the independence of the individual and his rebellion against supposed ultimate standards of authority.[1] Hence the impossibility of laying down a system of morality which shall be good for all time. And yet it is this socialistic element in morality which affords a basis for the ethics of supernaturalism, for

[1] For a concise account of the movement of ethical theories, see Mr. S. Alexander's *Moral Order and Progress*, book ii., chap. i. Trübner & Co.

there is a body of moral doctrine, an accumulated tradition of moral experience, against which it is impossible for the individual to rebel. The moral "atmosphere" or "spirit" into which we may happen to be born helps to mould and so limit our individual character. Thus we have, on the one hand, an authoritative standard, or body of doctrine, in morals, to which the individual feels bound to submit; and, on the other hand, we have the moral independence of the individual, which reacts on the body of doctrine, adds its little mite to the traditions of moral experience, and gradually purifies such portions of the moral atmosphere as are out of harmony with man's healthiest and highest aspirations. Any consistent theory of morals must necessarily take into account these opposing movements.

In this essay, however, as we are considering the sanctions of morality in their relation to religion, we must deal mainly with the individual. Let us, then, begin by asking: What is the distinctive feature of human character? And what are the highest and strongest incentives to moral endeavour? I think that the first, the fundamental axiom of humanitarian ethics, as distinguished from the ethics of supernaturalism, is that human nature, so far from being something inherently depraved, is in reality a noble and a beautiful thing, ever striving to reach higher altitudes of moral life. It is true, indeed, that we may find instances which seem to illustrate the depravity of human nature—instances, say, of wanton cruelty to innocent children. But these may be looked upon as exceptions which prove the rule.

Such conduct we rightly stigmatise as *unnatural* and *inhuman*, whilst to right and noble conduct we apply the contrary term—*humane*. It is this upward tendency of human nature which is its distinctive characteristic. But this upward tendency, or potentiality of improvement, implies an ideal of conduct or of life to which the ordinary self must stand in the relation of lower to higher. Hence, the incentives to moral endeavour must be found, not in man's personal happiness, either here or hereafter, but in the simple, yet natural desire to make the higher conception or rule of life prevail over, or usurp the place of, the lower. That is, the highest and most powerful incentive must be—love of the Ideal Good manifested, as of necessity it must be manifested, towards those with whom the word "good" implies relation—namely, our fellow-men. In this sense alone does the true meaning of Christ's words flash on our minds: "Inasmuch as ye have done it unto one of the least of these my brethren, ye have done it unto *Me*." In the hero and the martyr we see this exalted idea of duty manifested in its highest form; the aim of humanitarian ethics is to implant the same motive in every human heart. By large numbers of mankind, perhaps by the great majority, actions are performed merely because public opinion, or custom, requires their performance; and evil courses are avoided because the fear of social ostracism, or of losing caste with one's neighbours, acts as a deterrent. Those who are kept in the path of rectitude by these motives are on the same moral level as those who are influenced by hope of reward or fear of punishment. The ethics of the future must rise above all such motives, and must give us higher sanctions of morality. Just as, in the religious life, we seek to commune with the eternal source of things, so, in the moral life, we seek to render our lives in accordance with the highest good.

But whence, it will be asked, do we derive our ideas of what we consider to be the highest good? What is the arbiter which strikes us with compunction and misgiving, even if we momentarily deflect from the ideal line of conduct we have chosen for ourselves? Or, in other words, what is the standard by which we determine what is right and what is wrong? And immediately the answer comes to the humanitarian or evolutionist as to the supernaturalist—Conscience. But we have already seen that conscience is not always a reliable guide; that its dictates, in different individuals, not only often conflict with the prevailing conceptions of justice, but—what is more to the point—that it frequently inspires actions which the maturer and wiser judgment of humanity unhesitatingly condemns. Let us then try to ascertain how far conscience may be looked upon as a trustworthy guide. For this purpose it is necessary to ask ourselves, What is conscience? Without attempting to give a scientific definition of the word, it will be sufficient for our purpose if I define it as the sum of our inherited moral experiences by which we instinctively repudiate that which we believe to be wrong and cling to that which we believe to be right. That is, conscience may be said to bear the same relation to the moral faculties that instinct bears to the intellectual faculties. Thus the savage, without the aid of compass, strikes his way through the forest without a thought of the inextricable mazes in which the inexperienced traveller would soon lose his way; the migratory bird knows instinctively its way across the seas; the sick-room nurse moves about the sick-chamber with that instinctive gentleness of touch and motion which distinguishes her from the rough intruder who is unaccustomed to the ways of the sick-room: so the upright man has an instinctive repugnance to lying, theft, cruelty, and every kind of meanness. Just as the countless experiences of preceding generations find their temporary fulfilment in the bird or the savage, so the countless experiences of preceding generations endow the upright man with what may be termed moral instinct or conscientiousness. The barbarian of prehistoric ages may not have had any scruples respecting the practice of lying or of thieving, may indeed have looked upon such practices as duties in his relations with hostile tribes. But experience would show that these methods of wrong-doing ultimately resulted in unhappiness for the community, and consequently for the individual, whose happiness is in great measure bound up with that of the community. Thus a desire for truth would gradually spring up in the mind of the savage; as he progressed towards civilisation this desire would find embodiment in his religion, and so receive to him a kind of divine sanction, every succeeding generation and every triumph over falsehood giving strength to the inherited conscientiousness, until in our own day we find the impress so strong in many minds that truthfulness is looked upon as the first duty of man to man.

There are, indeed, many who would be willing to sacrifice themselves, if it were necessary, in the cause of truth or of justice, not from any intuitive feeling that such sacrifice would be in accordance with the Will of a personal Deity, but from the feeling—intuitive, if you will, in the sense of intuition arising from inherited experience—that their martyrdom would tend to the triumph of their cause and the ultimate moral elevation of the community. It is this consciousness of the binding force of man's relations to his fellow-men, giving precedence to the welfare of the community over that of the individual, which furnishes the sense of moral obligation, and gives us the real meaning of the word "ought." Whence does this consciousness come? it may be asked. It is impossible, and indeed unnecessary, in a paper of this character, to trace in further detail the genesis of the moral consciousness. It is perhaps sufficient to say that this sense of moral obligation was probably originally derived from parental affection and the ties of family life. As a mother would naturally quiver with indignation at the sight of injury done to her child, and the father would go forth to battle to protect his family and defend his home, so the growth of the same feelings would produce a sympathy for the children of others. Indignation at the sight of unmerited suffering would pass from the *particular* to the *general*, and the warrior, in obedience to the claims of friendship, would go forth to battle, not only to protect his family and his home, but also to defend his tribe from the attack of the enemy. That this derivation of the sense of moral obligation is perfectly natural we may see by a reference to the life of the lower animals. The bear, the dog, the bird, will not only defend their own young; they will, on occasion, unite for the purpose of defending others of their own species from attack. True, the sense of moral obligation here may not be so highly developed as in man; but the *germ* is there. If it is intuitive in the one case, it must be so in the other. The supernaturalists, and especially those—the great majority—who do not believe that animals have immortal souls, have to deal with the fact that some dogs are nobler than some men.

It may be objected that this theory is insufficient to account for the sense of moral obligation, that the gulf between the sanctions drawn from experience and those deduced from what is termed the intuitive recognition of the supremacy of the moral law, cannot be bridged, and that guidance by pleasures and pains fails to give us an ideal moral criterion by which to determine conduct. This objection, however, only re-introduces the metaphysical argument in another form, and brings up the question—whether ethics is prior to metaphysics, or metaphysics prior to ethics. Undoubtedly both sciences border upon each other, and there *may* be ethical questions which can only be solved by calling in the aid of metaphysics. But it would be illogical to infer from this that ethics is therefore necessarily a part of metaphysics. Moral actions—and it is these with which ethics has to deal—are usually performed without a thought of the metaphysical ideas which are implied in moral theories. The theologian would say that it is necessary to have some idea of the relation of man to God or to the universe before we can formulate a true ethical theory. But this is to read into the idea of conduct an element which it does not necessarily possess. In determining our attitude towards man we—unconsciously perhaps—determine at the same time our relation to God. Hence, moral action, *as* moral action, stands independent of metaphysics. As regards practical issues then—and here we are seeking only practical issues—the question as to the derivation of the sense of moral obligation need not further detain us. It is undoubtedly tempting to a certain order of mind to introduce metaphysical problems into ethical science, to consider metaphysics and ethics as inextricably bound up with each other, to systematise the whole mass of physical, metaphysical, psychological, and ethical phenomena, and to present to the world a ready-made theory of the universe, all spic and span. In reality, however, ethics rests on no such foundation. It bears much the same relation to metaphysical as to theological doctrine—it takes its stand upon the facts of conduct, and judges and interprets conduct by its relation to society as a whole, leaving metaphysics to form its own conclusions as to the relation of man to the universe. The development of the moral consciousness in man is a fact with which both metaphysics and ethics are concerned, but, in estimating the bearings of this fact, it is by no means necessary that we should go to metaphysics to find a religious sanction for moral judgments. To use the words which George Eliot puts into the mouth of Romola de' Bardi: "If everything else is doubtful, this suffering that I can help is certain; if the glory of the cross is an illusion, the sorrow is only the truer. While the strength is in my arm, I will stretch it out to the fainting; while the light visits my eyes, they shall seek the forsaken." In obedience, then, to this law of development, the upright man will strive to realise his highest conception of life, will regard the perfecting of his individuality, and, through this, the uplifting of the race, as his highest duty, and self-renunciation, when necessary for the good of others, as his highest ideal. Thus we see that it is not individual happiness or pleasure, in the material sense, or even utility—unless utility be taken to mean, as it was stated to mean by John Stuart Mill, the general rather than the individual good—it is none of these which forms the basal principle of humanitarian ethics; it is the desire to realise in conduct our highest conception of human life. Instead of moral endeavour being pitched on a low key, it must be pitched on a high key. And as in the old faith, "to him that ordereth his conversation aright shall be shown the salvation of God," and righteousness "shall bring a man peace at the last," so in the new faith the workers therein shall find that in striving to realise their highest conception of life there comes a spiritual, or perhaps I should say a refined, happiness. There is, indeed, a sense in which the two faiths, in their highest aspects, blend in one, and I fancy I hear the Christian moralist exclaim: "This is the teaching of Christ under another name!" If this is the case, may we not say that the teachings of Christ have been perverted by the Church, and that such doctrines as those of human depravity and eternal torment are the signs of a low stage of moral development?

Accepting, then, conscience as the foundation of the moral law, we are constrained to ask ourselves if this is a sufficient guide in all cases. We have already seen that it is, necessarily, an imperfect standard. In the diverse relations of life there are constantly springing up new situations and questions in the determination of which conscience is but one factor amongst others, situations in which we are perplexed as to which will be the right course to pursue. I do not mean that there should be any dallying with conscience where duty is clear and unmistakable. We instinctively feel, and reason gives confirmation to the feeling, that to be just should be our highest endeavour, but we are not always quite sure as to what constitutes justice. If, as will generally be granted, conscience is subject to the law of development, it can be a trustworthy guide only in a general sense: that is, we give a ready obedience to its dictates to be truthful and just, because the eternal rightness of such dictates has been verified in numberless experiences. But in the determination of the justice of particular courses of action, another factor, reason, must enter. The savage, though having some consciousness of duty to the members of his own tribe, would have no compunction in leaving a wounded member of a hostile tribe to die of hunger in the forest. But experience, aided by reason, would show the futility of interminable strife and hostility between tribes; peaceful pursuits would take the place of warlike; constantly repeated experiences would widen the range of cases to which the dictates of conscience would be applied, thus broadening or developing this faculty into a firmer, truer, and more general guide, until, to the most highly civilised men, conscience dictates that there should be no hostile tribes or nations, but that the whole of humanity should be one great brotherhood, each unit deserving of succour according to his need.

But let us take an illustration which will throw the question into clearer light. We all know how strongly the early Christian Fathers denounced the custom of usury—that is, the taking of interest on loans, however small the percentage. According to Mr. Ruskin and the Socialists, the Fathers of the Church were right, and modern society is all wrong. Here, then, in a case in which are involved the needs of our fellows, and our duties in face of those needs, conscience, with the great majority of people, is powerless; if appealed to, it fails to give any dictate, and leaves the settlement of the right or the wrong of the case to reason, and so we have a host of economists, from Bastiat to Mr. Henry George, demonstrating, to the satisfaction of themselves and the bondholders, that interest is perfectly just. Where the interest charged, however, is excessive, as in cases of bills of sale, conscience is often roused, and denounces it as "usury," but where the rate charged is what is termed "moderate"—the sweet simplicity of three per cent.—the average man pockets his dividends without scruple, and does not think of concerning himself with the question as to where "interest" ends and "usury" begins. It is quite possible, however, that, as a result of Mr. Ruskin's eloquent teaching and the pertinacity of the Socialists, the world may be brought round to their point of view, and, reason having then decided the question, we shall see conscience accepting a new moral standard—that is, becoming perfected by the accretion of new moral experiences. Instead of allowing custom to cloak its delinquencies under the pretext that it receives its dividends from the rich—the banker, the syndicate, or the joint-stock company—both reason and conscience will then aid in rousing dormant and inchoate sensibilities by pointing to the wretched lives of the individuals who create the wealth out of which interest is paid—the overworked and underpaid docker, tramguard, tailor, and seamstress. This, however, is only one case out of many. In the daily round of life we are continually being brought into situations in which the torturing question, "*Am* I doing right?" unanswered by the helpless conscience, paralyses effective endeavour, and we find ourselves thrown back on the judgments of reason.

We see, then, that conscience may be looked upon as the general criterion or standard of moral action, but that it is subject to continual modification and development; and further, that in the particular cases in which conscience can give only a general dictum—"Do the right"—reason is called in to aid in determining what is right. Here, however, we are brought to the vexed question of the freedom of the will and moral responsibility. If man is not responsible for his actions, then, indeed, morality, in the usual sense of the word, has no conceivable basis. We may blame or praise a man for taking a particular line of conduct, but our blame or our praise must be given with the object of preventing bad or inducing good conduct, as the case may be. If he is not responsible, he is not culpable, and we can no more apply the words "good" and "bad" to him personally, as implying merit on the one hand, or fault on the other, than we can apply the term "moral" to a tree. We can use such terms only in reference to the acts themselves and their consequences, not with reference to the *doer*. Still, it may not be out of place to point out that, after all—on the supposition that the will is free—human responsibility is confined to an exceedingly small number of actions, comparatively speaking. We have seen that man is not wholly responsible for his beliefs, and yet what a large number of actions spring from belief! Perhaps the only actions for which a person can be held accountable are those which he performs in opposition to his profound beliefs—that is, when he elects to obey the promptings of low or degrading motives in opposition to those which we term high or elevating. But even here large deductions are to be made. For a moment's consideration will convince us that every man's acts are very largely dependent on organic conditions. Inherited tendencies, prejudices, habits, and passions act on the mental organisation of every individual. Then, again, there are outward circumstances — temptations, immoral surroundings, imperfect training—in a word, environment: all these the moral faculty has to struggle against as best it may. We see, then, how little room there is left for moral responsibility. We say with an easy jaunti-

G

ness that lying and theft are wrong; but the moment we are brought to a concrete instance we are dumb — there is so much that we do not know, we feel ourselves in the dark, we suspend judgment. We punish the offender for his offence against the well-being of society; but at the bar of judgment none shall be his accuser, for none can know the depth and power of the inherited passions, motives, and controlling impulses which impelled him to action.

Despite these considerations, however, we are forced to the conclusion that to a certain extent, however small, man is morally responsible for his actions. The very element of consciousness leads us to look upon the determinants of the conduct of a man, and the determinants of the course of a tree or a stone—in which this element is of course absent — as wholly different in kind. We say that man has a power of reasoning, of deliberation, of fixing his attention on certain thoughts, of weighing and balancing motives, all which really constitute a power of self-control. And it is this power of self-control which denotes the *relative* freedom of the Will. This, at anyrate, we assume in our systems of training and education, and perhaps it would not be wise to follow the advice of the late J. Cotter Morrison, who, without mincing the matter, tells us that "the sooner the idea of moral responsibility is got rid of, the better it will be for society and moral education."[1] Nevertheless, we should do well to modify our theories of moral education, and approach the questions of human freedom and moral responsibility, not solely, as hitherto, from

[1] *The Service of Man*, p. 215. Third edition.

the general point of view, but from the standpoint of the individual. That is, the question should be, not whether the Will of man is free, but rather—what power of self-control has he? or, to what extent is character dependent on organic conditions and environment? Questions, the answer to which depends, in any given case, on the mental constitution of the individual concerned, there being, as already observed, inherited tendencies in each individual organisation, which tendencies limit volitional action, and make it, to a greater or less extent, the slave of innate passions and prejudices. Thus the evil-doer, impelled by momentary passion, or led into evil courses by inherited weakness or instability of moral character, cannot be said to be as free as one who has inherited a strong mental organisation, who can judge coolly and impartially, and who, by an effort of will, can check the flow of passion. Surely no one will contend that the drunkard who has inherited his craving for intoxicants from a race of debauchees, and whose will is powerless to resist outward temptations and innate cravings and impulses, is as "free" or as morally responsible for his actions as one whose character and organisation are untainted by such inherited tendencies. The same reasoning will apply to every phase of moral character. We do not think of judging those who are mentally weak, or those who are ignorant of the difference between right and wrong, by the same standard as that by which we judge those who are aware of these differences, and who are gifted with a strong mental organisation. All this seems to imply not only that the Will is relatively free, but that this freedom varies with varying mental organisation—the greatest power of deliberation, of self-control, giving in any given case the greatest conditional freedom.

But the moment we make the slightest concession to the doctrine of human freedom and moral responsibility, we are brought face to face with the law of causation. We are bound to believe that every event, mental or physical, is the effect of antecedent conditions. Neither are we much helped by the suggestion that the causation which obtains in the moral world is different in kind from that which obtains in the physical world. Causation is causation, whether applied to mental or to physical states. We cannot rid ourselves of the consciousness of "antecedent conditions," or what is termed "the cohesion of psychical states." If, then, the mental organisation is as subject to environment and the law of heredity as is the physical organisation—or, in other words, if moral evil is the result of moral disease, just as physical pain is the result of physical disease—why should we praise a man for being morally healthy, virtuous and heroic, any more than for being in sound physical health?

It has been maintained that the law of causation is not incompatible with moral responsibility. Professor Huxley, for example, in his work on Hume, says: "So far from necessity destroying moral responsibility, it is the foundation of all praise and blame."[1] And again: " A man's moral responsibility for his acts has, in fact, nothing to do with the causation of these acts, but depends on the frame of mind which accompanies

[1] *Hume*, p. 193.

them."[1] But, with all due deference to Professor Huxley, it may be asked, on what does the "frame of mind" depend? And if the "frame of mind" depends on inheritance—that is, has been transmitted, say to A, by preceding generations—how can it be said that manifestation of *caused* passion by A—the causes being admittedly outside his control—is morally wrong, or that he "ought" to control it? Professor Huxley wishes, apparently, to close the controversy by giving a narrow definition of the word "liberty" as applied to volitional actions, for he approvingly quotes Hume thus: "By liberty, then, we can only mean *a power of acting or not acting according to the determinations of the will*; that is, if we choose to remain at rest, we may; if we choose to move, we also may. Now, this hypothetical liberty is universally allowed to belong to every one who is not a prisoner and in chains. Here, then, is no subject of dispute."[2] But this definition the advocates of the doctrine of free-will will by no means accept. It is merely tantamount to saying that the physical organisation has power to register or carry into effect the decisions of the mind, which, indeed, no one doubts. But this is not the question. Neither Hume nor Professor Huxley goes far enough back. The question is not whether we have a power to register mental decisions by outward action, or, in other words, "a power of acting or not acting according to the determinations of the will," but rather—Is the will free to determine *what* acts the physical organisation shall enregister? I can,

[1] *Hume*, p. 192.
[2] *Ibid.* pp. 190, 191.

if I choose, raise my hand. That none will dispute. But the raising of my hand is the result of a mental decision. That mental decision is arrived at, or is caused, by some prior consideration, say the present discussion. The same holds good even if, after all, I do not choose to raise my hand. The chain of causes is unbroken. The question, then, is this—Can the will be said to be free when any given mental decision is the result of a series of determining causes *some of which lie outside the range of consciousness?* And if the will is not free, if mental decisions are formed *for* man and not *by* man, how can he be said to be morally responsible for those decisions, or for the acts consequent on them? This is the problem which has never been solved.

But our difficulties do not end here. They surround the advocate of the doctrine of free-will as completely as they surround the necessarian. Let us grant for a moment that an uncaused volition is conceivable— which it clearly is not—then surely such a volition cannot be held morally accountable any more than an imbecile or a demented person can be held accountable for his vagaries. Professor Huxley well observes that "the very idea of responsibility implies the belief in the necessary connection of certain actions with certain states of the mind. . . . If a man is found by the police busy with 'jemmy' and dark lantern at a jeweller's shop door overnight, the magistrate before whom he is brought the next morning reasons from those effects to their causes in the fellow's burglarious ideas and volition with perfect confidence, and punishes him accordingly. And it is quite clear that such a proceeding would be grossly unjust if the links of the logical process were other than necessarily connected together."[1]

On this point Professor Clifford is still more emphatic. "To deprive us of the scientific method [with reference to human action] is," he says, "practically to deprive us of morals altogether."[2] And in enforcing this contention, he says: "Let us endeavour to conceive an action which is not determined in any way by the character of the agent. If we ask, 'What makes it to be that action and no other?' we are told, 'The man's Ego.' The words are here used, it seems to me, in some non-natural sense, if in any sense at all. One thing makes another to be what it is when the character of the two things are connected together by some general statement or rule. But we have to suppose that the character of the action is not connected with the character of the Ego by any general statement or rule. With the same Ego and the same circumstances of all kinds, anything within the limits imposed by the circumstances may happen at any moment. I find myself unable to conceive any distinct sense in which responsibility could apply in this case; nor do I see at all how it would be reasonable to use praise or blame. If the action does not depend on the character, what is the use of trying to alter the character?"[3] In support of his argument Professor Clifford quotes Sir William Hamilton as follows:

[1] *Hume*, p. 192.
[2] *Right and Wrong: the Scientific Ground of their distinction;* a Lecture, p. 33.
[3] *Ibid.* pp. 30, 31.

"Nay, were we even to admit as true, what we cannot think as possible, still the doctrine of a motiveless volition would be only casualism; and the free acts of an indifferent are, morally and rationally, as worthless as the pre-ordered passions of a determined will. . . . . That, though inconceivable, a motiveless volition would, if conceived, be conceived as morally worthless, only shows our impotence more clearly. . . . Is the person an *original undetermined* cause of the determination of his will? If he be not, then he is not a *free agent*, and the scheme of necessity is admitted. If he be, in the first place, it is impossible to *conceive* the possibility of this; and in the second, if the fact, though inconceivable, be allowed, it is impossible to see how a cause, undetermined by any motive, can be a rational, moral, and accountable cause."[1] In spite of this clear statement of the case, however, Hamilton affirms that the scheme of necessity is inconceivable, because it leads to an infinite non-commencement, and that the possibility of morality depends on the possibility of liberty; for if man be not a free agent he has no moral responsibility at all. All which, if it shows nothing else, certainly shows the very dense mental fog we are all in.

In what relation, then, must humanitarian ethics stand to the question of human freedom and moral responsibility? First of all, such a system of ethics must take its stand upon the facts of consciousness, however irreconcilable these *appear* to be. Recognising the uniformity of nature in human action as well as in the outward physical world, and the fact that,

[1] *Ibid.* pp. 31, 32.

under any circumstances, man's character is largely dependent on the influences of heredity and environment, it will hesitate to pronounce judgment upon the culpability of any action, and will give due attention to the suitability of environment for producing certain types of character. Instead of relying upon the will as the sole or even the principal instrument of moral reformation—as a sincere believer in the doctrine of the freedom of the will is logically bound to do—it will give primary attention to the education of the moral and intellectual faculties, or, in other words, to the cultivation of human nature. On the other hand, it will also recognise the fact that there is a vital difference between causation in the physical world and causation in human thought and action, between the determination of non-sentient things by outward causes and the determination of living and reasonable beings—a difference occasioned by the very fact of consciousness. A stone is determined by purely external causes; a rational being is determined by internal as well as external causes. The impelling powers or influences of external causes may be said to centre or converge in the mind of man; the mind has power to review, to weigh, to consider them; it thus becomes itself a *factor* in the ultimate determining cause. Hence arises the power of self-control. The mind, properly educated, fixes its attention upon a given object, and keeps that object in view as the end to which it will attain. By this means bad habits may be gradually but slowly overcome and good ones formed. Here is a basis, however narrow, for moral self-improvement. There is a kind of restricted or conditioned freedom which, as I have already said, varies with each individual; some, with weak will, being apparently the mere quips and sports of fate; others, with stronger will, holding themselves well in hand, weighing motives, controlling impulses, guiding passions, directing conduct.

This, then, must be the relation of humanitarian ethics to the questions of causation, human freedom, and moral responsibility—that the law of causation, or uniformity of nature in human action as in physical phenomena, is an undoubted fact; that self-control is a factor in causation and implies a conditioned freedom of the will; that moral responsibility, in varying degree, springs from this power of self-control; and that, therefore, it is the duty of society to so order the environment of the individual that outward causes shall tend to produce the highest type of character, such types, by increasing power of self-control, attaining greater relative freedom of volition. This, of course, does not in any sense pretend to be a reconciliation of the doctrines of freedom and necessity, but is merely a statement, in the light of present knowledge, of the relation of ethics to important psychological questions affecting our judgment of human conduct. The solution of the problem—if it ever can be solved —must be left to the wider knowledge of a more enlightened age.

And now we can return to the consideration of our main thesis. We have already seen that conscience must be regarded as the general criterion of moral conduct, but that it is subject to continual modification and development. We have seen also that reason is a determining factor in the evolution of conduct. And, in addition to the promptings of conscience and the voice of reason, we may add another factor which often over-rules the dictates of reason—that is, sympathy, or emotional feeling. Some moralists have regarded sympathy not merely as an element entering into the formation of conscience, but as the basis of the moral sense. That there is a vital difference between the two is, I think, quite clear. Conscience may be said to be that which has to do with the rightness or wrongness of thoughts and actions, and is imperative in its character, while sympathy is that quality which is called forth independently of the higher processes of thought, and is characterised by a natural feeling of affection or attraction, rather than by a power to formulate imperative dictates. We instinctively shudder at the sight of cruelty, without a mental reference either to conscience or to reason to ascertain whether our sympathetic feeling towards the sufferer is based on right and adequate grounds. That sympathy requires conscience and reason as aids and correctives in the determination of conduct is apparent, for it is frequently the case that when the grounds of punishment become known, sympathy is diverted from those who are undergoing punishment to those who are inflicting it. Sympathy, then, may be regarded, not as the basis of the moral sense, but as one of the "collateral associations" which go to the formation of conscience; hence the necessity for giving it its due place in the development of character and the determination of conduct.

Thus we have, without any need for reference to

the ethical theories of supernaturalism, a sufficient, and, as far as in the nature of the case lies, a complete natural guide to moral conduct. To those who wish for an infallible authoritative standard of morality, the theory outlined in this essay will appear inadequate for the guidance of man. But an *infallible* authority fallible man cannot possess. The first acceptance of any standard by the human mind must be, to a large extent, dependent on reason and observation, and these, in their turn, on the varying mental states of different individual minds, thus introducing at once the element of fallibility; if its acceptance is not dependent on reason and observation, then it is evidently based on unverified assumptions.

Having thus shown the basis of what may be termed the internal or subjective sanctions and impelling motives to moral endeavour, it remains for us to point out the principal outward or objective stimuli, which, in their turn, impel man to consider the good of others independently of the consequences to himself. Space will not allow me, nor perhaps is it here desirable or necessary, to trace the growth of the altruistic feelings in man. Both John Stuart Mill and Herbert Spencer have, I think, clearly demonstrated the natural connection which exists between egoism and altruism, and have shown how the welfare of the individual is bound up with the welfare of all,[1] the idea of individual interest thus naturally expanding and developing until it generates the idea of family, tribal, and collective interest, and lastly, the idea

[1] See Mill's *Utilitarianism*, chap. v., and Spencer's *Data of Ethics*.

of the welfare of humanity. " By virtue of his superior intelligence, even apart from his superior range of sympathy, a human being is capable of apprehending a community of interest between himself and the human society of which he forms a part, such that any conduct which threatens the security of the society generally is threatening to his own. The same superiority of intelligence, joined to the power of sympathising with human beings generally, enables him to attach himself to the collective idea of his tribe, his country, or mankind in such a manner that any act hurtful to them rouses his instinct of sympathy, and urges him to resistance."[1] The idea of human welfare needs only to be reinforced by a simple fact in nature to furnish every needful external or objective stimulus to moral endeavour, and the only needful incentive to realising the highest ideal of moral life; the fact—which indeed is a mere truism, but is nevertheless in the moral life frequently ignored —that cause and effect are indissolubly interlinked, that every thought, every word, and every action leaves its indelible impress not only on our own lives, but on the lives of others also; every single thought and action being the root, as it were, of other thoughts and other actions, and these influencing other and future lives for ever in ways of which we have no conception. And further, every thought and every action produces its corresponding good or evil effect. Even if it be a mere fleeting and momentary desire, the stir of a secret impulse, which vanishes ere it breaks into outward action, that impulse is woven

[1] Mill's *Utilitarianism*, p. 77. Eleventh edition.

into the very texture of our being, and produces its influence in our own life, and so on surrounding individuals; or, by the law of heredity, its effect is transmitted, through us, to the after-generations to whom we impart our life. Thus, what has been well termed "the solitary life of the soul" is as much a matter of concern to the humanitarian as it is to the orthodox theologian. We need not the inspiration of faith to tell us that the fruit of our service to humanity will be eternal; we know this to be the unalterable course of nature. Every thought and every action has either a good or an evil influence! A sanction for morality? Here is the divinest sanction! Is it, indeed, of no consequence to each one of us that our deeds carry with them joy and gladness, or, on the other hand, that they bring sorrow and suffering in their train? Is it of no moment that our suffering brothers and sisters appeal to us, even though indirectly, in vain? Can we, in our wrong-doing, stifle the accusing voices which rise to remind us of what we *might* have done in the opportunity which has gone for ever? Nay, not so. We know in our heart of hearts, because we have been taught by bitterest experience, that the fruit of selfishness, bringing misery and perhaps death to others, is ashen in our hands as we grasp it; whilst the fruit of righteousness is imperishable as the amaranth, giving promise eternal of living power and beauty for others, and, perchance, containing within itself the potency of richest and highest life for ourselves. "The fruition of our service is eternal!" This is the watch-cry of the higher morality. For if any man dare to stand on the brink of futurity and commit an action which he knows will have an evil influence, that man at once brands his conscience with the indelible impress of conscious wrong-doing, and his act and its consequences form his own condemnation. For he elects corruption rather than purity, evil instead of good, darkness instead of light, the fleeting illusions engendered by the gratification of the lower self, in place of the enduring verities of truth and justice. Time is the recording angel, and eternity is the book; every thought and every action are graven in that book, neither are there any erasions there, save those which are slowly worn away by the hidden sufferings and secret sorrows of those who have to purge their souls of the evil influence.

Thus do we find our sanctions of moral endeavour, simple, clear, and unmistakable, in the needs of our common humanity. The calls of our fellow-men are imperious and commanding, and the necessity for obedience will remain as long as sorrow and suffering shall endure:

> "Hath man no second life? *Pitch this one high!*
> Sits there no judge in heaven our sin to see?
> *More strictly, then, the inward judge obey!*
> Was Christ a man like us? *Ah! let us try*
> *If we, then, too, can be such men as he!*"

Saddened and oppressed by the silence of the Eternal, we feel the greater need for sympathy and communion with the human. And who knows but that in this way alone we may ultimately attain to communion with the Supreme? 'Blessed are the pure in heart, for they shall see God!" Strange how some of the most beautiful sayings of Christ, read by the light of the doctrines of the New Reformation, become clear to our minds, fraught with a truer, a higher, a holier meaning! "Purity in heart"—that is the spirit of God manifested in human life, and the Kingdom of Heaven is indeed "within" us.

CHAPTER V.

THE NEW REFORMATION AND ITS RELATION TO SOCIAL PROBLEMS.

THERE are many points of resemblance, though not of a superficial character, between the period of transition through which we are now passing, and the struggle which convulsed the nation in the early part of the seventeenth century. And not the least striking of those points of resemblance is this—that both movements are the outward and palpable embodiment of the Puritan spirit in man revolting against the corruptions which beset the religious ideal, and waging war against the moral deadness of the world, engendered, in the one case, by the wildness and licence which accompanied the Renaissance, and by the shameless immorality of the Church; in the other, by the sordid and demoralising influence of our economic and industrial system. Both are alike as typifying a rebellion of the human mind against traditional authority—one, rebellion against the authority of the Church; the other, rebellion against the authority of a creed. But both differ in this—that while the one sought the embodiment of its religious ideals in the *political* reorganisation of society, the other seeks the realisation of those ideals in the *social* reorganisation of society. But the true point of resemblance lies in the fact that the foundation and impulse to action of both movements, of the Puritanism of our forefathers as of the Puritanism of to-day, is the religious spirit in man.

Let it be noted, however, that by the word "Puritan," I mean the Puritan spirit as distinct from the Puritan faith. And the Puritan spirit knows no distinction of sect. It may be exemplified in the life of a George Herbert as in that of a Richard Sibbes, in a Falkland or a Verney, as in a Hampden or a Cromwell. But in Herbert and Falkland we see the Puritan spirit in repose; in Sibbes and in Hampden we see the Puritan spirit in action. In the former, we have what Matthew Arnold would term the "perfect balance," which culture alone can give; while in the latter, we have a development of only one side—the religious side—of life. The principle, however, for which Mr. Arnold does not make sufficient allowance, is this—that extremes necessarily call forth extremes; hence, where extreme licentiousness or irreligion prevails, the militant religious spirit will ultimately spring into being as a counteracting force. When a nation has sunk to the lowest depths of degradation, when the principles which it professes with its lips find no response in its heart, when, wrapped in selfish and slothful ease, it hears not the call of the sufferer and listens no longer to the cry of the distressed, then, indeed, is needed—to use the words of Mr. Ruskin—"the earnest purity of the girded loins and the burning lamp" to bring men back to the higher life, to awaken them to renewed devotion to duty, to restore the vanished ideal. *Then,* kid-glove warfare and light-rapier fencing are unequal to the task before them. The needs of the time necessitate stern and bitter conflict, heroic devotion, self-sacrificing life, and though the religious side of man may as a consequence be abnormally developed, it is so developed that it may the more effectually grapple with the evils which have called it into existence. Hence do we see at the present time a revival of the militant Puritan spirit—but a Puritanism divorced, as I have already said, from the old Puritan faith—a spirit which is everywhere manifesting itself in an intense dissatisfaction—nay, shall I not say a determined spiritual revolt against a social order which, in its worship of Mammon, is materialistic to the core.

There are, then, at present in the world of thought, two great movements slowly developing and progressing side by side. One may be said to be predominantly intellectual, the other predominantly emotional. The former, helped in its momentum by the philosophic thought of men like John Stuart Mill, Mr. Herbert Spencer, and Professor Green, by the scientific research of men like Darwin, by the literary genius of Matthew Arnold and Ernest Rénan, and by the Biblical criticism of a host of German workers, takes shape under the name of the New Reformation; the latter, assisted in its development by the early labours of Robert Owen and by the teachings of Carlyle, Kingsley,[1] and Mr. Ruskin, and

[1] I say "*assisted* in its development." I need not, of course, stay to explain, that though the teachings of Carlyle and Kingsley have unconsciously helped forward the socialistic forces of the age, those teachings differ widely, in many respects, from our modern scientific Socialism, for which, possibly, Carlyle and Kingsley would not have had much sympathy.

marked by the rise of a new school of political economy, which, in its theoretic aspects, has likewise been influenced by German thought, stands forth under the somewhat indefinite name of Modern Socialism. Both movements have influenced, though in varying degree, almost every section of religious thought and life. The Churches, both National and Nonconformist, have unconsciously absorbed the spirit of the age in its diverse manifestations—we have not only a Christian Socialism in our midst, we have also an Agnostic Christianity. But the very fact that the spirit of the age, as expressed more particularly in advanced religious thought, has been to some extent absorbed by the Churches, makes the present a most critical time for the further development of the movement known as the New Reformation. Critical in this—that the negative or destructive period in advanced religious thought is rapidly passing away, and the time for constructive work has begun. If anyone dispute this, let him note the significant change which has come over the great mass of the people during even the last decade. Now, the great question is, not "What shall I believe?" but, "How shall I live? How can I best realise my ideal of human life?" As evidence of this change amongst the working-classes I may point to the decline of the Secularist movement. Secularism may be said to have been almost exclusively a working-class movement. Ten or twelve years ago it was at the height of its success, but its propaganda was purely destructive. Now that the need for destructive work is rapidly passing away, and having no constructive mission peculiar to itself, Secularism is simply a dying movement. Many of its most earnest workers have left its ranks to devote their energies to the constructive work to be found in Radical and Socialist causes. And what is true of the working-classes is equally true of every other portion of the community. Philosophic thought, scientific research, and Biblical criticism have, in this respect, done their work. Almost unconsciously, men are beginning to assume the progressive development of religious thought and life, independent of the *form* which religion may take; independent, also, of the spontaneous dissolution of theological systems of belief.

It can no longer be doubted, then, that, whether for good or ill, a large proportion of thinking people have, in a religious sense, broken the old bonds. The dogmas which were instilled into our minds as Biblical truths have, for many of us, been transformed into beautiful legends, and, through doubt and confusion, we have at last emerged from what we now regard as the rigid exclusiveness of doctrinal creeds and customs. But whether, on that emergence, we proceed to worship, with Mr. Herbert Spencer, at the altar of the Unknown God; whether, with Matthew Arnold, we seek to place ourselves in the current of that "stream of tendency by which all things seek to fulfil the law of their being;" or whether, with Thomas Hill Green, we look upon God as immanent in man rather than as an objective reality, upon Christ as the Divine Exemplar rather than as the incarnation of the Supreme, and upon Heaven as a condition—the realisation of one's ideal self—rather than as a place;

whichever of these mental attitudes we are led to adopt, our religious life cannot end here—that is, in the mere intellectual appreciation of a given philosophic or religious truth. Having attained, in some measure, to what Mr. Arnold terms "spontaneity of consciousness," it is necessary that we look to its Hebraistic converse—"strictness of conscience." Our social and moral endeavour must be the expression, the embodiment, of our religious faith. Hence, the moral and religious fervour which has hitherto expressed itself in what we now believe to be inadequate forms and methods of worship, must be diverted into the more effective channels of human sympathy and love. Hence, too, the reason why the New Reformation, as a constructive movement, is now, or will shortly be, on its trial.

But though we have severed ourselves from orthodox Christian faith and doctrine, it is impossible to cut ourselves aloof from Christian tradition. That tradition, obscure though it may be in its details, is clear and palpable enough in its main outlines. The greater sanctity of human life, the need of self-sacrifice when the common welfare is endangered, the brotherhood of man, these were the ideas which Christianity, in its highest manifestations, forced upon the attention of mankind. But how far is that tradition in actual operation and influence in the Christianity of our own time? Is it not evident on every hand that there has been a complete divorce between the highest dictates of Christian ethics and the customs and practices of our so-called Christian society of to-day? Were I asked to give an example of that divorce I would point to the industrial and business life of the nation. Instead of "bearing one another's burdens and so fulfilling the law of Christ," it appears to be the aim of everyone to push his burden on the back of someone else. The custom of buying in the cheapest market and selling in the dearest—which may be interpreted as getting as much as one can out of one's fellow-man and giving as little as one can in return, independently of all considerations of justice—this custom, although the almost universal rule of a Christian business community, is in direct antagonism to the teachings of Christ. But we shall the more readily estimate the completeness of that divorce if we glance for a moment at the work of the early Catholic Church and note the manner in which it attempted to apply the socialistic teachings of the Gospels to the actual life of the people. That the teachings of Christ and the apostles *were* socialistic it recognised and accepted without question, instead of conveniently ignoring that fact as the Protestant Church has done. The early Christian fathers boldly applied those teachings to economic life. The practice of buying cheap and selling dear was condemned; the clergy were absolutely forbidden to engage in trade; goods were to be sold at a "just" price, and every detail of sale was to be regulated according to the strictest moral principles. In addition to this, usury, *i.e.*, the taking of interest, *however small the percentage*, was looked upon as a sin. Usurers were visited with ecclesiastical censures; later, they were treated as heretics, and were liable to be proceeded against by the inquisitors; and, ultimately, through the teaching and influence of the Church, the secular authorities instituted legislation against the practice. But the very spirit of history was against the Church. It is, of course, manifestly impossible to deal in this article with the economic forces which gathered themselves against her. One of those forces may, however, be summed up in two words—material progress. The discoveries of the early navigators not only widened the mental horizon of man, they stirred in him the passion for the possession of a share of the enormous wealth which those discoveries disclosed. The wonderful stories of returned travellers stimulated the instinct of greed. Trade and commerce took a wider range and sweep, and the inventive genius of man revolutionised the old system of wealth-production. This development of industry from exceedingly simple to complex methods and customs brought tasks to which the Church, even if it had not been beset by other difficulties and dangers, was bound, from its very lack of experience, to prove unequal. But these other difficulties and dangers assisted the economic forces, and of these difficulties, the Reformation was the chief. The rise and establishment of Protestantism, though it produced inestimable benefits, not the least of which was the assertion and development of individuality of thought, lost to the world, in that very assertion, the pure ethical teachings of Christ, of the apostles, and of the early fathers. In asserting and maintaining the *rights* of conscience in matters of belief, it failed to imbue the mind with a due sense of the corresponding *duties* of the individual in matters of conduct. To the historian of the future the rise of modern industrialism and the reign of *laissez-faire* must be the veritable dark age of Protestantism, for no one can turn to the study of the social condition of the people during the pre-factory-act era without a shudder at the heartless cruelty, slavery, and degradation which then prevailed. But it was, perhaps, impossible that progress in ethics could keep pace with material and intellectual progress. Man lacked the necessary experience for applying a high standard of morality to the new social and industrial problems which so rapidly arose. Now, that experience has been gained. Social conditions and material progress have themselves begun to force upon man the duty, nay, the necessity, of harmonising economic with true ethical doctrine.

We are now, perhaps, in a better position to ask ourselves, What is the attitude which the New Reformation must assume towards the industrial and social problems of our time? Now that it has settled its religious convictions and is passing from the negative to the positive stage of its work, what is its aim and mission? To the present writer, at any rate, the answer comes clear and unmistakable,—it must place itself in direct and sympathetic contact with that great social movement which seeks to transform the industrial and business life of the nation, to animate that life with a moral motive, to lift it to a higher level. While engaging in those practical schemes for the alleviation of human misery which the exigencies of time and circumstances demand, it must also devote itself to the social work which has a wider range and deeper basis. That is, it must deal with causes rather than with effects; it must strike at the roots of the social upas rather than at the branches thereof; it must place justice before philanthropy. Hence, while establishing Elsmere Institutes, it will recognise these —useful and excellent though they may be—as mere palliative and temporary expedients for the brightening of the bleak places in which human life is cast. Behind, or, rather, above all, it will place the realisation of that social ideal in which the great mass of the people shall have the leisure and the opportunity to make the best possible use of themselves, to devote themselves to the higher pursuits and aims of life, to cultivate and develop their highest individuality; in a word, to promote that general harmonious expansion of the faculties which is what we mean when we speak of human perfection. That, I say, and nothing less than that, must be the aim of any movement which dignifies itself with the name "religious." Just as Christianity was an attempt to introduce a higher moral ideal into human life, just as the Reformation was an attempt to render that ideal of greater effect in the actual life of the people, so, every new expression of religious thought and life, even though it first manifest itself in the dissolution of old faiths and beliefs, is, in like manner, an attempt to embody or realise those nobler conceptions and ideals which are the offspring of a higher humanity. Hence, religion has a social aim. Without that social aim, without high moral endeavour, it is a vapid, selfish thing, devoid of backbone, and apt to degenerate into that barren formalism which, lacking both vitality and earnestness of purpose, is the mere skeleton of religion.

But in what manner must the New Reformation set itself to accomplish that aim? First, by bringing the moral and religious spirit into direct contact with the economic and industrial life of the nation. It is this separation of religion from the conduct of daily life which is at the root of the great problem of increasing poverty with material progress, of intellectual and material advancement outstripping the growth of the moral sense. Undoubtedly, one of the main causes of this separation is to be found in the teachings of the Church. Directing the attention of man to things supernatural, and regarding belief in certain theological dogmas and metaphysical propositions, which are incomprehensible by the average mind, as of primary importance, conduct—which, as Matthew Arnold has told us, makes up three-fourths of life,— has been looked upon as of merely secondary signification, and moral endeavour has thus been mis-directed, and its efficiency thereby impaired. Hence the divergence between the Christianity of our own day and the Christianity of Christ. Our first work, then, is to restore the Christianity of Christ, to free his personality from the myths and legends which have hitherto surrounded it, to give to the world a higher, because a truer, conception of his life and a more faithful interpretation of his teachings, and to show that the *spirit* of those teachings is applicable to our economic and social life of to-day. Here, again, we may turn for warning to our orthodox Christian society, or to Christianity as it expresses itself in our modern civilisation, and note how falsely the whole life and mission of Christ has been interpreted by the orthodox world. For what is the dominant feature of our Christian civilisation? Is it not a base scramble, or, at any rate, an inordinate desire for material possessions? Is it not the weakness of orthodox Christianity, as expressed in the social life of its adherents, that it has, generally speaking, laid hold of the things which are of least value—wealth, position, and power—and has entirely missed the things which are of most value in human life? We know, of course, that the whole life and teachings of Christ and of the apostles are quite opposed to such an interpretation as our so-called Christian civilisation implies, that those teachings require us to look upon wealth and position—material possessions—as of secondary, nay, of quite insignificant value. But we have no need to appeal to civilisation for our warning; we need only look around us, at the daily life and conduct of our orthodox friends. Let us take, for example, the main supporters and representatives of our religious establishments and institutions—State and Nonconformist. Of the first, we may surely take our land-owning aristocracy as the most substantial supporters and representatives; and of the average member of our land-owning aristocracy may we not say, generally speaking, that he is the peculiar and highest product, and practical exemplification, of our materialistic Christianity—one who looks upon wealth and position and power as the main things of life. For though he is what is termed a man of culture—but of culture as understood, as Matthew Arnold would have said, only in a restricted sense, one who has cultivated only one side of his nature—he goes to church and listens, with a complacency which would be quite amusing were it not for its disastrous social consequences, to such texts as: "Bear ye one another's burdens," and, "He that will not work neither should he eat;" the simple matter of fact being that he is all the while increasing other people's burdens by the exaction of what is wrongfully termed "unearned increment," an "increment" which is certainly not earned by the landlord, but which, nevertheless, flows into his pockets to the amount of hundreds or thousands or scores of thousands of pounds per annum as the case may be, and which is unmistakably *earned* by downright hard toil —toil of hand, and body, and brain, which whitens the hair and furrows the face and saddens the heart—performed, possibly, while the landlord is listening to an exposition of the beatitude—"Blessed are the poor in spirit!"

And now, on the other hand, let us take the main supporters and representatives of those other religious establishments which may be grouped together under the name of Nonconformist, and which are united by the bond of the Liberation Society. Who, for example, are the pillars—I mean the solid and substantial, not the rhetorical pillars—of the Liberation Society? Are they not chiefly to be found amongst the wealthy tradesmen and merchants and manufacturers of our large towns? And do we not find that their interpretation of New Testament teaching, their view of true religious life, is quite as wide of the mark as we find the interpretation of the main representatives and supporters of the Established Church to be? Are they not, of all people in the world, the very class of people who make wealth and position and power—including, of course, occasional chairmanship of a tea-meeting—their chief aim in life? Their fundamental business principle is to buy cheap and sell dear, or, in other words, to get as much as they can from their neighbour and give as little as they can in return. It is a matter of supreme indifference to "Plugson of Undershot," whether he buys a bale of cotton, a piece of cloth, or a human life, so long as he can make a profit out of it, for increased profit means, of course, an increase in the very things which he regards as of most value in life. He has no scruples in paying his workmen the magnificent remuneration of twenty or twenty-two shillings per week for work which is calculated to wear out body and soul by the age of thirty-five or forty years, while he himself takes care to receive a princely income for work which is calculated not to wear out *his* body until he is sixty-five or seventy years of age. And though he has often read—and perhaps still oftener heard—the story of Christ's temptation by Satan, and has a dim apprehension of the meaning of the text about gaining the whole world and losing one's own soul, he would be dumfounded were those passages of Scripture applied to himself. And so he takes for his guidance in life —or, rather, for the guidance of his business life, which is the foundation of his moral and social life— a principle which is the very reverse of the Golden Rule, and literally does unto others that which he would *not* have others do unto him!

Here, I say, is our note of warning. I do not need to be reminded that our social evils are far too complex to be removed by appeals to the individual conscience and personal character of men; that our economic and industrial system is itself full of anomalies which tend to neutralise the effect of such appeals; in short, that "system" is as much responsible for our social evils as is "character." But let us not forget that character lies behind the system. The very basis of our life, the impelling spirit of all endeavour, is the inner, personal, *ethical* life, and I have dwelt the more insistently upon this side of the question, because it seems to me that this is the point of contact between that wave of advanced religious thought which is now passing over the world—the New Reformation—and the great social upheaval of our time. Perhaps the one thing which, more than any other, has driven the masses away from the Church, is the travesty of the teachings of Christ which the orthodox world has presented, by actual practice and example, to the observation and for the imitation of men. "If these," the masses have in effect said to themselves, "if these—our pastors and masters—are the professors and representatives of Christ's teaching; if this—our present industrial and social system—is the outcome of that teaching, then Christianity is not for us;" and they have turned sorrowfully away to a religion of indifferentism and despair. Here, then, is the field for that constructive work which must distinguish the New Reformation from all purely sceptical movements; this is the task which it must set itself to accomplish—the realisation of a higher ideal of individual and social life. Making conduct, instead of creed, the test of life, it will apply that test to the industrial and business relations of men, and so infuse into our system of wealth production and distribution, a moral motive; in other words, it will make its highest conception of justice the standard for the regulation of our economic life.

It was once an axiom in a certain school of political philosophy that religion should be kept distinct and separate from political life, as being a man's individual and private business, with which the world had no concern. That may have been true when religion was thought to consist in the holding of certain speculative opinions which had no perceptible or direct influence on human conduct. But that time is past. To the words "religion" and "religious" we have given a wider, a deeper signification, and we now say that life and conduct must be the palpable expression, the outward embodiment, of religious faith. Having won our battles for political and religious freedom, we are sometimes content to rest on our laurels and to forget our differences in the call for a wider fellowship. Let us take care, however, that the fellowship be not too wide, and that it shall not admit the pseudo-philanthropist who sends his cheque for five hundred pounds to this or that charitable institution while his workmen are existing on starvation wages. It is one of the defects of orthodox Christianity that it is spasmodic in moral endeavour, devoting its efforts to the surface instead of to the roots of social evils. Hence, the equanimity with which Dives *creates* suffering on the one hand, by accepting or extorting wealth to which he has no moral right, and attempts to alleviate it on the other by the salve of a one-hundred-pound subscription; hence, the insistence by the clergy on the duty of charity. In the higher Religion, however, justice must precede charity. Handsome donations to the building of churches—even of its own churches—it will regard, not with gratitude, but with suspicion, meeting such with the stern query: "Who has been defrauded of his inheritance?" For the guidance of our pastors and masters in this connection, I need only quote the words of Mr. Ruskin: "Let the clergyman only apply —with impartial and level sweep—to his congregation the great pastoral order: 'The man that will not work, neither shall he eat;' and by result in requiring each member of his flock to tell him *what*—day by day— they do to earn their dinners; and he will find an entirely new view of life and its sacraments open upon him and them. For the man who is not—day by day—doing work which will earn his dinner, must be stealing his dinner; and the actual fact is, that the great mass of men calling themselves Christians, do actually live by robbing the poor of their bread, and by no other trade whatsoever; and the simple examination of the mode of produce and consumption of European food—who digs for it and who eats it—will prove that to any honest, human soul."

For those of us, then, who have enlisted under the standard of the New Reformation,—" labourers of the new seed-time, whereof the harvest shall be not yet," —duty, individual and social, becomes clear and imperative;—individual, in the realisation of our highest ideal of human life; social, in the application of our highest conception of the moral law to the economic and industrial life of the people, so that everyone may have the means and the opportunity for the development of his highest individuality, for the attainment of a wider mental horizon, a deeper insight into the problems of life. Though cutting ourselves aloof from orthodox Christian doctrine, we may continue that high tradition which runs like a golden thread throughout history, rising above all doctrinal excrescences, and, by the martyrdom of the noblest spirits of humanity,—martyred by the Faith as well as for the Faith,—carrying mankind to higher levels of life. If, while discarding the doctrines, we continue to imitate the practices and customs of the orthodox world, we are but as Pagans " suckled in a creed outworn,"—a " sad Fraternity, whose faith and hope are dead." But this I cannot believe. Strength of purpose, purity of passion, high moral enthusiasm, are perennial in the human heart. Faith dies, to rise renewed to sterner fortitude; Hope perishes, to be revived by visions of an ampler life. It is ours to revive that hope, to rekindle that faith, not by restoring the dreams of a heavenly paradise, but by the consecration of our service to the realisation of that earthly paradise which must be the reward of human endeavour.

CHAPTER VI.

THE TRUE TEACHERS OF THE WORKING CLASSES.

TEN or twelve years ago it was the fashion amongst political thinkers to regard English Socialism as a movement of foreign importation—the mere echo of the economic theories of German collectivists like Ferdinand Lassalle and Karl Marx, or of the social doctrines of French theorists like Saint-Simon, Fourier, and Louis Blanc. Even Mr. John Rae, in his *Contemporary Socialism*, published in 1884, expressed the opinion that there was "no sufficient reason for believing that Socialism had secured any serious foothold in England."[1] Now, however, everything is changed. The air is full of socialist watchwords. Socialist organisations, or branches of existing organisations, are multiplying with remarkable rapidity. The New Unionism is deeply tinged with the socialistic spirit; even the steady-going co-operative movement has become infected with socialistic ideas; and, what is of even greater significance, a considerable section of the educated middle class is beginning to see that a competitive system of society is, to say the least, an inadequate and unhealthy milieu for the development of the higher human virtues. What, then, is the cause of this rapid development of public

[1] P. 59.

opinion, this remarkable change in the attitude, not only of the working classes, but of all sections of society, towards Socialism and social problems? To say, nowadays, that Socialism is a movement of foreign importation, or that it has "secured no serious foothold in England," would betray a profound ignorance of modern industrial and political life, and the tendencies of modern economic thought. To the working classes, outside London at any rate, Marx's *Capital*—which, in Germany, has been called the Bible of the working classes—is as a sealed book; Louis Blanc's *Organisation du Travail* is absolutely unknown; and Lassalle, Proudhon, Fourier, and Saint-Simon are mere names. It is perfectly true that these theorists, especially the first named, have had a distinct influence on English thought—an influence which plainly manifests itself in socialist literature, and which, by this means, percolates into the working-class mind. It is also true that there is a school of Socialism in England which pins its faith to Marx's *Capital*. But the Marxian economics have never taken any real hold of the English mind. Even amongst the most active and influential section of English Socialists, there is a decided difference of opinion as to whether Karl Marx supplies the true key to the solution of the economic problem. To what source, then, shall we look for the genesis of this great outburst of socialist activity? If, as I have said, the movement is no foreign importation, but is, in its main characteristics, of English origin, then we must look to our own literature, and the progress of our own national life, for the causes of its growth and development.

It is, then, to the slow evolution of the "time-spirit," or, in other words, to the stern pressure of economic circumstance, that we must look for one of the main causes of the growth of Socialism amongst our English workers. The story of the Industrial Revolution, that period of stupendous enterprise and energy, of marvellous invention, of ever-extending commerce and almost boundless increase of wealth, and also, let it be added, of extreme poverty, degradation, and even slavery for the working classes, that story, I say, is an old one, which need not be repeated here, but it is a story which has sunk deeply into the hearts of the English people. The period of the Industrial Revolution, and more especially the latter part of that period—1800-1830—may, as far as the actual condition of the people was concerned, be called the Dark Age of English Protestantism. Human labour, divested of soul, was regarded simply as a commodity to be bought and sold like a bale of wool, and human life, from the age of seven upwards, as an instrument for the satisfaction of one of the basest passions in human nature—the greed for gold. It was in this period that the seeds of English Socialism were laid, and these seeds showed their first fruits in the Socialist movement founded by Robert Owen. But Owen, though right in his economic principles, not only miscalculated the forces against which he had to contend, he mistook the means by which those forces were to be overcome. Had he been able to establish his self-governing communities on a permanent basis—which was, in the nature of things, impossible—they would but have continued as isolated experiments managed by a community of the faithful. The force of example may be great, but the force of experience is greater, and it is in the bitter school of experience that the English democracy has learned many of its socialistic lessons. Owen was the inventor of a system, and it is not by systems that mankind is reformed, it is by development from within.

But both the Owenite and the Chartist movements were significant as showing the tendency, in the first half of the nineteenth century, of the current of intelligent working-class opinion. Both movements were socialistic—the one voluntary in its methods; the other, political, aiming first, like its modern prototype, at the control of the State by democratic machinery. But the time was not ripe for the full fruition of either movement. The thinking minds of England were still in the grip of the old economics and the *laissez-faire* school of politics. It may be contended that the Factory Acts were a protest against the doctrines of *laissez-faire*. A protest, doubtless, but not a self-conscious one. No; the Factory Acts were passed not through any conscious revolt on the part of the nation against the school of *laissez-faire*, but, as Mr. John Rae points out, "from practical motives of humanity, bent on relieving distressed classes of the population from the sufferings they were seen to endure."[1] The *conscious* revolt in literature came later; in economics and practical politics it began with Mr. Gladstone's Irish Land Act of 1881. Let us turn for a moment to the economists of the period of the Industrial Revolution, and

[1] *Contemporary Socialism*, p. 392.

we shall then be able to see more clearly what that revolt really means, for it is here that we meet with the real clues to the development of modern Socialism.

In the history of economic thought, from 1770 to 1830, three names stand out clearly and distinctly—Adam Smith, Jeremy Bentham, and David Ricardo. Smith's *Wealth of Nations* was published on the eve of the Industrial Revolution, and in it we see how the author was dominated by the idea which had taken possession of the thinking minds not only of England, but of Europe,—the idea, nay, the passion, for individual liberty. The atmosphere was alive with the political theories which ultimately culminated in the French Revolution. Man's energies had been cramped, his aspirations thwarted, his outlook circumscribed, by the mediæval theories which still retained their influence in legislation and social life. It was to escape this influence that the people sent forth a great cry for political emancipation, for individual freedom, for "natural liberty." It was this doctrine of natural liberty that Adam Smith applied to economics. Industry and trade were hampered by a host of legislative restrictions, and it was these that the author of the *Wealth of Nations* sought to remove in order to give scope for the development of industry through the operation of unrestricted competition. But Adam Smith was not merely a political economist, he was a philosopher, and his economic theories were but deductions from his philosophic doctrines, or, at any rate, his economics were profoundly influenced by, and bore the impress of, those doctrines. Fundamentally, his theories were much the same as those of the physiocratic school—both advocated what is termed the "system of natural liberty." Nature, in her order and her method, was to be the schoolmistress of man. "Little else is requisite," wrote Smith, "to carry a State to the highest degree of opulence from the lowest barbarism, but peace, easy taxes, and a tolerable administration of justice; all the rest being brought about by the natural course of things."[1] And again: "Projectors disturb Nature in the course of her operations in human affairs; and it requires no more than to let her alone, and give her fair play in the pursuit of her ends, that she may establish her own designs."[2] The same principles underlie the economic doctrines set forth in the *Wealth of Nations*. "Every individual," he says, "is continually exerting himself to find out the most advantageous employment for whatever capital he can command. It is his own advantage, indeed, and not that of society, which he has in view. But the study of his own advantage naturally, or rather necessarily, leads him to prefer that employment which is most advantageous to the society."[3] And again: "The individual generally, indeed, neither intends to promote the public interest, nor knows how much he is promoting it. By preferring the support of domestic to that of foreign industry, he intends only his own security; and by directing that industry in such a manner as its produce may be of

[1] Quoted by Dugald Stewart in Introductory Memoir to the *Wealth of Nations*, p. 13. (Ward & Lock's reprint of 1812 edition.)
[2] *Ibid.* p. 12.
[3] *Wealth of Nations*, book iv., chap. 2.

the greatest value, he intends only his own gain, and he is in this, as in many other cases, led by an invisible hand to promote an end which was no part of his intention. Nor is it always the worse for the society that it was no part of it. By pursuing his own interest he frequently promotes that of the society more effectually than when he really intends to promote it."[1] These were the principles which, though not explicitly presented as such, were the real foundation of the Smithian system of economics. And these doctrines were reinforced, in politics and morals, by the Benthamite school, and again in economics, by Ricardo. The result was seen in the attitude of the philosophic radicals on labour questions. So long as legislation was designed to throw off all restrictions on industry and competition, it received their ardent support, but the moment it proposed to touch the sacredness of "freedom of contract"—*i.e.*, the right of the wealthy and the powerful to drive a hard bargain with the poor and the weak—it met with their unflinching opposition. And this, although the philosophic radicals were singularly humane men, sincerely and earnestly desirous of elevating the great mass of the people. Thus Hume, in proposing the repeal of the Combination Laws in 1824, grounded his argument on the right of the workman to combine in order to meet the tyrannous exactions of the employers—"their property," he said, "enabled them to get the better of the men." Yet, in obedience to his philosophic principles, he declared, in opposing the Factory Bill of

[1] *Ibid.*

1833, that "all legislation of this nature is pernicious and injurious to those whom it is intended to protect, and I have not the slightest doubt that if this Bill should continue in operation five years, it will have produced incalculable mischief. It must be the interest of the masters to protect their workmen, and it is a libel upon human nature to suppose that they will allow persons in their employment to be injured for the want of due caution." The socialist answer to this — coming, strange to say, from the lips of a Tory, Michael Thomas Sadler—was complete. "The boasted freedom of our labourers," he said, "will, in a just view of their condition, be found little more than nominal. Those who argue the question on mere abstract principles seem, in my apprehension, too much to forget the condition of society, the unequal division of property, or rather, its total monopoly by the few, leaving the many nothing whatever but what they can obtain by their daily labour, which labour, however, cannot become available for the purpose of daily subsistence *without the consent of those who own the property of the community*, all the materials, elements, call them what you please, on which labour is bestowed, being in their possession. Hence, it is clear that the employer and the employed do not meet on equal terms in the market of labour; on the contrary, the latter, whatever his age, and call him as free as you please, is often almost entirely at the mercy of the former."[1]

But the theories — which, after all, were but theories—of Adam Smith, crystallised, in the hands of

[1] See Toynbee's *Industrial Revolution*, p. 19.

Ricardo, into immutable "laws." This it was that completed the triumph of *laissez-faire*. To divest human nature of its noblest attributes, to regard man solely as an economic instrument for making money, to look upon self-love as—to use the words of Malthus—a divinely-appointed attribute for the regulation of human conduct, by which "the most ignorant are led to promote the general happiness,"[1] and to invest the deductions from these principles with the character of irrevocable law, as dangerous to interfere with as the laws of the physical universe, was an achievement which placed the industrial world entirely at the feet of those who would have made love of power and greed for gold the dominant passion of the race. The world was indeed ready, not merely in a physical, but in a spiritual sense, for the enactment of the great drama, or shall I not say the tragedy, of the Industrial Revolution. The political economists, the philosophic radicals, the Whigs, the manufacturing and merchant classes, and the Press which echoed, and still echoes to some extent, the teachings of the old political economy—were united, though from different motives, in their opposition to the demands of labour; and the working classes, defeated in their attempt to gain control of governmental machinery through the Chartist agitation, could only wait for the inevitable reaction against the soulless teachings of the economists. Happily, that reaction had already begun to manifest itself. If Adam Smith, Bentham, and Ricardo had, more than any other three individuals of their time, the greatest influence on the legislative policy of the nation, during

[1] *Principle of Population.* Appendix, p. 448, vol. ii. (1807).

the first half of the nineteenth century, there are three others who—leaving aside for the moment John Stuart Mill, whose teaching was distinctly transitional in its character—have had the greatest influence on the thought of the latter half of our century, and that influence will undoubtedly bear fruit in future legislation. These three are Carlyle, Ruskin, and Matthew Arnold. It is in *Sartor Resartus* that we discern the first signs in literature of the great reaction against *laissez-faire*, and the revival of that transcendentalism which is the spiritual nursing-mother of socialistic theories. Carlyle's teaching is often condemned as being largely of a negative character, and it is no doubt true that his writings are mainly a criticism of existing opinions and institutions. But his phrases have become the watch-words of the modern socialist movement. " A fair day's wage for a fair day's work ; " " Permanence of employment ; " " Organisation of labour," —these are positive enough in implication if not in themselves. Even his negations imply affirmations which are distinctly socialistic. The denunciations of *laissez-faire* imply, for example, the duty of government to legislate in accordance with a certain ideal of social life. " Call ye that a society," says Teufelsdröckh, " where there is no longer any social idea extant; not so much as the idea of a common home, but only of a common over-crowded lodging-house ? Where each, isolated, regardless of his neighbour, turned against his neighbour, clutches what he can get, and cries ' Mine ! ' and calls it peace, because, in the cut-purse and cut-throat scramble, no steel knives, but only a far cunninger sort, can be employed?"[1] It is in such passages as these, in his commentary on the eighth commandment, which, he says, "has all but faded away from the general remembrance, and, with little disguise, a new opposite commandment, thou *shalt* steal, is everywhere promulgated, and the widest and wildest violations of the divine right of property are sanctioned and recommended by a vicious Press, and the world has lived to hear it asserted that *we have no property in our very bodies, but only an accidental possession and life-rent;*"[2] in his frequent insistence on the duty of justly apportioning the wages of work done, and on the need for the governmental organisation of labour—" the problem of the whole future,"—it is in such passages as these, I say, that Carlyle shows his detestation of the principles of the old political economy, and shows also his entire sympathy and accord with many of the socialistic aspirations of our time. For what is the real meaning of the just apportionment of wages to work done—" the everlasting right of man?" It is neither more nor less

[1] *Sartor Resartus*, book iii., chap. v.
[2] *Ibid.* book ii., chap. x. The ordinary middle-class reader who has forgotten his *Sartor*, may think that Carlyle was referring to those journals which advocate the nationalisation of the land, mines, railways, and the instruments of production. Not at all. He was referring to the ordinary party newspaper which justified, on the then accepted principles of Political Economy, the theft of this social wealth from the workers, and the consequent oppression of the latter by the manufacturing and trading classes, through the application of the precepts of a "shabby mammon-gospel of supply-and-demand competition, *laissez-faire*, and devil take the hindmost."

than, in general terms, the socialist demand that the reward of labour shall be fixed and regulated, not by competition, but by the moral sense of the community; or, in other words, that payment for work done—like our daily conduct to our next door neighbour, but with far greater reason—shall be regulated by the moral law. "The progress of human society consists even in this same, The better and better apportioning of wages to work. Give me this, you have given me all. Pay to every man accurately what he has worked for, what he has earned and done and deserved,—to this man broad lands and honours, to that man high gibbets and treadmills: what more have I to ask? Heaven's kingdom, which we daily pray for, *has* come; God's will is done on earth even as it is in heaven! This is the radiance of celestial justice; in the light or in the fire of which all impediments, vested interests, and iron cannon, are more and more melting like wax, and disappearing from the pathways of men."[1] But the suggestion that every man in the State, who does his work conscientiously and well, should have at least a fixed minimum wage which would be sufficient to keep his wife and family in decency and comfort, is enough to take away the breath of the average politician and the employer of labour. "What is to become of our trade?" they ask in amazement. To which I may give the reply which Carlyle gave to the manufacturers, who, on the introduction of the Factory Bill, exclaimed, "What is to become of our cotton trade?" "Let your cotton trade take its chance. God Himself

---

[1] *Past and Present*, book i., chap. iii.

commands the one thing; not God especially the other thing. We cannot have prosperous cotton trades at the expense of keeping the devil a partner in them!"[1] And this is exactly the contention of the Socialist— that if a given industry will not support existence in decency and comfort, let the industry perish. But, of course, Carlyle's answer is insufficient, and he knew it. And so he insists upon the Government organisation of labour—which is neither more nor less than the socialistic demand for national or municipal workshops —in order that, by abolishing the private landlord and capitalist, and so facilitating a just division of the produce of the nation and a saving of the enormous amount of waste labour caused by needless competition, neither home nor foreign trade might suffer.

Perhaps the one instance in which Carlyle appears to run counter to the tendencies of modern thought is his deification of the hero and his contempt for the machinery of democratic government. But even in his attitude on these questions there is a certain amount of truth, though that truth is obscured by a good deal of talk about the futility of ballot-boxes, winnowing-machines, Reform Bills, and the like. We all know that new truths always begin with minorities, that the majority, if not " mostly fools," is largely composed of the average man, who can see no further than the end of his nose, and that there is the greatest difficulty in the world in selecting, through this majority, by the process of counting noses, a government of the wisest and best. But with all Carlyle's contempt for ballot-boxes, it is evident to

[1] *Past and Present*, book iv., chap. iii.

the most superficial reader of his works that this is the weakest point in his political philosophy. He has nothing whatever to offer in place of the ballot-box, while his own account of the election of Abbot Samson simply shows that the method supposed to be adopted was even more hazardous than our present popular method of election, and as Dr. Garnett observes, "proves that the choice might as easily have fallen upon some tonsured 'Pandarus Dogdraught.'" But even Carlyle himself seems conscious of the weakness of his own position on this matter, admitting, as he does, the importance of electoral methods. "It is a most important social act; nay, at bottom, the one important social act. Given the men a People choose, the People itself, in its exact worth and worthlessness is given. . . . A People's electoral methods are, in the long-run, the express image of its electoral *talent;* tending and gravitating perpetually, irresistibly, to a conformity with that."[1] What is this but a paraphrase of John Stuart Mill's dictum that "the worth of the State is the worth of the individuals composing the State." One might as well rail at the constitution of the universe as cavil at democracy for going its own way, instead of obeying, like dumb, driven cattle, the behests of some leader, or hero, or party. It is true, indeed, as Carlyle and Ruskin so often urge, that obedience should come before liberty, that it is an indispensable condition of true liberty; but that obedience must be to some higher authority which moulds the spirit from within, not to an external authority which makes the spirit its slave. After all,

---

[1] *Past and Present,* book ii., chap. vii.

one cannot help thinking that Carlyle's attitude on this matter was due to the eccentricity of his genius, to the intensity and strength of his individuality. The truest and best elements of his social teachings are to be found, not in his expressed contempt for democratic machinery, but in his insistence upon fellowship as the indispensable basis of human society, upon the recognition of the moral law, rather than competition, as the regulator of the reward of industry, and upon the collective organisation of labour as the true solution of industrial problems—all marking the pathway by which human nature may be led to a fuller and nobler development. It is in these things that Carlyle leads the great reaction against *laissez-faire*, competition, and the doctrines of the old Political Economy.

Turning now to the second great teacher of the working classes—John Ruskin—we shall find that, equally with Carlyle, he is a true exponent of the spirit of the age. Though he professes himself a disciple of Carlyle,[1] he is, in many respects, Carlyle's superior, for where Carlyle merely criticises the old order and leaves his criticism to germinate in the mind of the reader, Mr. Ruskin steps in and boldly lays down positive doctrines and principles in place of the old political philosophy, and new methods of organisation and polity in place of the old economic and industrial institutions. Mr. Ruskin sounds the key-note to his economics in the first sentence of *Unto this Last*, a book which, he tells us, he "believes

[1] See *Crown of Wild Olive*. Appendix.

to be the truest, rightest-worded, and most serviceable he has ever written." "Among the delusions which," he says, "at different periods have possessed themselves of the minds of large masses of the human race, perhaps the most erroneous—certainly the least creditable—is the modern *soi-disant* science of political economy, based on the idea that an advantageous code of social action may be determined irrespectively of the influence of social affection." It is upon the influence of the social affections, and the impulses, motives, and ideas to which these affections give rise, that Mr. Ruskin bases his economic theories. Just as domestic economy consists in the wise ordering of the affairs of the household, so political economy consists in the wise and just ordering of the affairs of the nation; and thus, as the good housewife will husband her resources to meet the time of stress and trial, administering the affairs of the household with gentleness and justice towards each member, suffering herself rather than see her charges suffer, so the wise State will administer the affairs of the nation with justice to its humblest citizen,[1] and so husband its

[1] It may be well to remind the reader, that in speaking of the State administering justice, Mr. Ruskin does not mean that kind of justice which is associated with the name and the methods of the law; he means that justice which consists in the fair and just reward for work done, the standard of such fairness or justice being fixed by the moral sense of the community, as an approximation to absolute justice—a much closer approximation than is the standard of competition. The just payment of labour really forms the starting-point of justice—*that* wrong, everything else is wrong, and the so-called justice of the law becomes a mere travesty, because the fountain-head itself is tainted.

resources and garner its wealth that even in times of scarcity and bad harvests none may pine for want of food and clothing, but all rejoice in the abundance of plenty. These principles Mr. Ruskin sets forth in no half-hearted manner, and, as stepping-stones to their ultimate realisation, the measures which he advocates are exactly those which now find a place in the Socialist programme. "Perhaps one of the most curious facts in the history of human error is the denial, by the common political economist, of the possibility of regulating wages irrespectively of the demand for labour; while, for all the important, and much of the unimportant, labour on the earth, wages are already so regulated."[1] What is this but the Socialist demand for a minimum wage to be fixed by the State? In addition to this, however, Mr. Ruskin would establish, as the first step towards the thorough organisation of industry, municipal training schools for the industrial education of the youth of the nation; secondly, and in connection with such schools, municipal workshops and manufactories "for the production and sale of every necessary of life, and for the exercise of every useful art;" thirdly, he would provide that any persons out of employment "should be at once received into the nearest government school, and set to such work as it appeared, on trial, they were fit for, at a fixed rate of wages, determinable every year;" and lastly, that pensions should be given to the aged, as a well-earned reward for so many years of labour.[1] These, almost word for word, are the main points in the Socialist programme now placed before the country

[1] *Unto this Last*, p. 18. Second edition.

by the Socialist organisations and the Trades Union Congress.

But these are only the surface facts of Mr. Ruskin's teachings. The great debt which the working classes owe to him is for the immense services which he has rendered in dispelling the false assumptions of the old political economy, in attacking the low ideals of commercial and industrial life, and in insisting upon the recognition of the truth that real wealth consists, not in heaps of hoarded gold, but in the fulness, the wisdom, and the nobleness of life. This he has done with a beauty of thought and language unequalled by any other prose writer of our century. Mr. Ruskin is far dearer to the heart of the English workman than is Carlyle. There is something about Carlyle—about both his personality and his style—which repels us. With all his depth of emotion and tenderness of feeling he is too bitter in his denunciations, too harsh in his judgments, too contemptuous of our failings and shortcomings; and, above all, he is out of sympathy with our democratic aspirations. Mr. Ruskin is far gentler both in tone and language, more charitable in his judgments, more considerate towards our shortcomings, though none the less stern in his condemnation of our backslidings. No working man can read the last sixteen pages of *Unto the Last* without experiencing a feeling of gratitude, and even of affection, for the man who wrote them. Even Mr. Ruskin's extravagances endear him to us, showing, as they do, the warmth and depth of his nature; but, unfortunately, it is his extravagances and eccentricities

---

[1] See Preface, *Unto this Last.*

which have misled the ordinary reader—and especially the newspaper reader—as to the real character of his teaching. Take, for example, his tirades against machinery. The common notion is that Mr. Ruskin condemns *all* machinery. Yet, every careful reader of his works knows that that is a notion which he explicitly contradicts.[1] What he does condemn is the excessive use of machinery in our daily life and work, tending, as it does, to cramp and deaden man's artistic instincts. Mr. Ruskin is, before everything else, an artist in whose theory of life Art is essentially related to Religion, and therefore to the soul of man. Anything which tends to develop the soul, to enlarge and ennoble its powers of activity, to fit it for a sphere of intenser and fuller life, must be fostered and developed; while anything which tends to dwarf these powers of activity, to sear the artistic instincts, to cramp the soul and to fetter its energy, and so destroy or debase its life, must be condemned. This, in brief, is the *raison d'être* of Mr. Ruskin's diatribes against machinery, and, whether we agree with him or not, we can easily see, when we become acquainted with his point of view, that there is much to be said in its behalf. This is scarcely the place, however, in which to enter upon a defence of Mr. Ruskin's eccentricities. My purpose is accomplished if I have shown the reader how strongly Mr. Ruskin's teachings are influencing the social and political tendencies of our time.

It would perhaps raise a smile of incredulity, and

[1] *Fors Clavigera*, vol. viii., Letter I.

would doubtless bring upon me the trenchant criticism of Mr. Frederick Harrison, were I to assert that the apostle of "sweetness and light" has had any direct and permanent influence either on the thought of the working classes, or on the development of the socialistic tendencies of the age. And yet, without committing myself definitely to the former proposition—inasmuch as Matthew Arnold's influence has, as yet, been mainly confined to the middle, rather than to the working classes of society—I may point out that Mr. Arnold professed himself an apostle of culture not merely for the sake of culture, but because an apostle of culture is necessarily an apostle of equality, or, as he himself expressed it, because "culture seeks to do away with classes; to make the best that has been thought and known in the world current everywhere; to make all men live in an atmosphere of sweetness and light. . . . This is the *social idea;* and the men of culture are the true apostles of equality."[1] Or again, "civilisation is the humanisation of man in society. Man is civilised when the whole body of society comes to live with a life worthy to be called *human,* and corresponding to man's true aspirations and powers. . . . First and foremost of the necessary needs towards man's civilisation we must name *expansion.* The need of expansion is as genuine an instinct in man as the need in plants for the light, or the need in man himself for going upright. . . . Inequality thwarts this vital instinct, and being thus against nature, is against our humanisation,"[2] and, therefore, against

---

[1] *Culture and Anarchy,* p. 31. Popular edition.
[2] Preface to *Mixed Essays.*

civilisation. It is scarcely necessary to say that Mr. Arnold does not mean absolute equality—that is, of course, impossible. He means a nearer approach to equality in the economic conditions of life, which will tend to promote true individuality, or, as he himself expresses it, that harmonious expansion of the faculties which makes for perfection. And what is the argument which Mr. Arnold makes use of in support of his contention? "The strongest plea for the study of perfection," he says, "the clearest proof of the actual inadequacy of the idea of perfection held by the religious organisations, expressing, as I have said, the most widespread effort which the human race has yet made after perfection, is to be found in the state of our life and society with these in possession of it, and having been in possession of it I know not how many hundred years. We are all of us included in some religious organisation or other; we call ourselves, in the sublime and aspiring language of religion, which I have before noticed, *children of God*. Children of God;—it is an immense pretension!—and how are we to justify it? By the works which we do, and the words which we speak. And the works which we collective children of God do, our grand centre of life, our *city* which we have builded for us to dwell in, is London!"[1] And this is exactly the argument of the Socialist. "And *this*," says the Socialist—though with not quite the serenity, urbanity, and facility of expression of Arnold—"*this* is the result of our religion and our civilisation." The accent on the "this" is significant enough.

[1] *Culture and Anarchy*, p. 20. Popular edition.

But it is in his sympathy with the Hellenic idea of the State that Matthew Arnold shows how largely he is in accord with the socialistic spirit of the age; and it is here, also, that he is at one with the teachings of Ruskin and Carlyle. "Liberty is a divine thing," says Carlyle, "but 'liberty to die by starvation' is not so divine." And this is what Arnold says too, but in different language. Readers of *Culture and Anarchy* will remember the chapter entitled, "Doing as one Likes," in which the author assails the old doctrines of *laissez-faire*, and pleads for the recognition of the State as the reflection of our best self. And here I am reminded of a sentence of Joubert's, which Mr. Arnold makes use of in his delightful essay on the gifted but sensitive Frenchman, and which really contains the pith of the whole matter—"In all things let us have justice, and then we shall have enough liberty." Justice *in all things*. Yes, that is what the labouring classes want. Not merely the justice of our law courts, but a new and higher ideal of justice, which will ensure an equitable share of the annual produce of the nation to the humblest citizen of the State.

> "And these all labouring for a lord,
> Eat not the fruit of their own hands;
> Which is the heaviest of all plagues,
> To that man's mind, who understands." [1]

Few men have done more than Matthew Arnold to undermine those false ideals of the middle and upper classes—the ideals of material wealth and worldly prosperity and power—of "getting on in the world,"

[1] *The Sick King in Bokhara.*

of "doing as one likes" so long as that means having a good balance at one's bankers—which have done so much to bring about the present unjust distribution of wealth. He has irritated them—or rather, such of them as are sensitive and refined enough to be irritated—out of their overpowering desire for riches and the false social esteem which riches bring, out of their vulgarity of temper and disposition, out of their narrowness of mind and aim. "The ideal society," he says, "what is it? It is the Kingdom of God upon earth." And the Kingdom of God—for Mr. Arnold—may be summed up in the phrase, "Sweetness and light;" for Carlyle, in the word "Duty;" and for Ruskin, in the word "Beauty." How, then, shall we attain unto the Kingdom of God? By following, says Mr. Arnold, the line of Jesus. "And undoubtedly the line of Jesus is: 'How hardly shall they that have riches enter into the Kingdom of God!' In other words: 'How hardly shall those who cling to private possession and personal enjoyment, who have not brought themselves to regard property and riches as foreign and indifferent to them, who have not annulled self and placed their happiness in the common good, make part of the ideal society of the future!'"[1] And "the ideal society of the future" is close upon us. Even now, as in the time of Christ, the "end of the age" is at hand. "Sometimes we may almost be inclined to augur that from such 'end of the age' we ourselves are not far distant now; that through dissolution—dissolution peaceful if we are virtuous

[1] *A Comment on Christmas*, see *St. Paul and Protestantism*, popular edition, p. 169.

enough, violent if we are vicious, but still dissolution—we and our own age have to pass, according to the eternal law which makes dissolution the condition of renovation. The price demanded, according to the inexorable conditions on which the Kingdom of God is offered, for the mistakes of our past, for the attainment of our future, this price may perhaps be required sooner than we suppose, required even of us ourselves who are living now: 'Verily I say unto you, it shall be required *of this generation.*'" [1]

These, then, are the teachings which are at present permeating the working-class mind, and which are aiding the development of the modern Socialist movement. I do not, of course, wish it to be inferred that the bulk of the working classes are at present eagerly studying Carlyle, and Ruskin, and Arnold. I wish they were. But there cannot be the slightest doubt that these teachers are influencing the most intelligent section of the working classes, and it is the more intelligent who influence the rest. There are in all classes, says Mr. Arnold, natures, "sown more abundantly than one might think, that set up a fire which enfilades, so to speak, the class with which they are ranked;" that is, which enfilades or impregnates the mass with the new ideas of the time. These ideas they communicate by conversation, by discussion, by lectures, by newspaper reading, by the constant contact of mind with mind. The life of the nation is influenced, not so much by direct contact with the highest literature, as by contact with the minds which

[1] *Ibid.* p. 171.

literature itself influences, and by the slow percolation of new ideas, new thoughts, new aspirations, into the intellectual life of the mass. And our labour leaders have become possessed with these new ideas, thoughts, and aspirations. They may be somewhat Philistine in their notions, they may be apt to give undue prominence to their class self, they may sometimes show a want of politeness and urbanity in their style and methods of advocacy, but then, not being men of culture, they cannot always fight, like Mr. Arnold, in kid gloves. It is true, too, as Mr. Arnold points out, that we may be too fierce in our hatred of the past, too Jacobinical in our ways of dealing with existing institutions, too severe in our judgments of the middle and upper classes. But then, Mr. Arnold, born and reared in an atmosphere of "sweetness and light," had never been the victim of the cruelty of the past, the iron of poverty had never entered his soul, he had never felt the terrible injustice of class ascendancy and class oppression. And that cruelty and injustice no man can conceive who has not felt it and lived under it, —felt it, not so much in the pressure of outward circumstance, as in the chilling and paralysing effect of an atmosphere which blunts the keener sensibilities, sears the finest instincts of the soul, and cramps and thwarts the energies of the mind. Our cry is a cry for *expansion*—the great need of the human spirit— in order that, by the refinement of our holiest instincts and the development of our highest faculties we may feel, with acutest sensibility, the glow and thrill of this vivid, pulsing, mysterious thing called *Life*.

It may be objected, as Mr. John Rae objects in his *Contemporary Socialism*, that the evident decline of *laissez-faire* does not mean the establishment of Socialism, and that "the State may become social reformer without becoming socialist." The distinction between the two is a difficult one to draw, but I think no careful observer of recent industrial and social developments will deny that the tendency of things is distinctly set in the direction, not merely of social reform, but of Socialism,—that is, the application of a new moral standard in estimating the value of human labour, or, in other words, the realisation of a higher ideal of justice in the apportionment of the wealth which is created by the community. The more extreme Socialists, indeed, might argue that this is not Socialism; that Socialism really means the adoption of some pet system of their own. But cut-and-dried systems never take hold of the life of a nation. The nation may, and often does, adopt what is good in a system, but it leaves the framework of the system to be nursed by the doctrinaire. Neither is our English political life favourable to the adoption of systems. The present phase of the socialist agitation amongst the working classes is proof of this. The labour candidates who are at present fluttering the dovecotes of party politicians, are, in many cases, men of socialist principles, but they know that it is the wisest policy to keep their more advanced tenets in the background until the electorate is sufficiently educated to deal with social and labour problems, irrespective of the convenience of either of the great political parties. And the labour leaders are rapidly awakening to the necessity for such education, and also to the necessity for a thorough political organisation of the forces at their command. It is a mistake to suppose that these leaders are representative of the great bulk of the working classes, but they are undoubtedly representative of the most energetic and intelligent section of their class. The great force they have to contend against is the conservatism—I use the word in its widest sense—of the older unionist and non-unionist workmen. It is well known that many of the former are averse to political action on independent lines, and are unwilling to spend their funds in political propaganda, while the great majority of the latter are still wedded to the old political parties. This is the true explanation of the check, if, indeed, it can be called a check, which the Labour movement has received in several constituencies in late elections. So far from being disheartened by that check, the Labour party is more than ever determined to take an independent course, and to educate the electorate in the principles of Trade Unionism and Socialism.

Add to these facts the further consideration that the more cultured portion of the middle classes is becoming distinctly influenced by socialistic ideas, and that the Church itself has been impregnated with the desire to realise a higher conception of justice, has at last found, that, to use the words of the Bishop of Durham, "its mission is to hasten a Kingdom of God on earth . . . to seek a new social application of the Gospel,"[1] and no dispassionate observer can doubt that

[1] Paper read at the Church Congress, Hull, October, 1890.

we are nearing the dawn of a new era. Society is passing through one of those critical, transitional periods which, as John Stuart Mill points out in summarising the Saint-Simonian philosophy, form the natural prelude to a new order. The history of the human race, said the Saint-Simonians, may be divided into organic periods and critical periods. "During the organic periods mankind accept with firm conviction some positive creed, claiming jurisdiction over all their actions, and containing more or less of truth and adaptation to the needs of humanity. Under its influence they make all the progress compatible with the creed, and finally outgrow it; when a period follows of criticism and negation, in which mankind lose their old convictions without acquiring any new ones, of a general or authoritative character, except the conviction that the old are false. The period of Greek or Roman polytheism, so long as really believed in by instructed Greeks and Romans, was an organic period, succeeded by the critical or sceptical period of the Greek philosophers. Another organic period came in with Christianity. The corresponding critical period began with the Reformation, has lasted ever since, still lasts, and cannot altogether cease until a new organic period has been inaugurated by the triumph of a yet more advanced creed."[1]

We are, I say, nearing the dawn of another positive or organic period. The most cherished beliefs, the most sacred faiths, the most venerable institutions, have been thrown into the crucible of criticism, and out of the alembic there must emerge new truths and

[1] Mill's *Autobiography*, pp. 163-4.

nobler ideals, which will lead mankind to the realisation of a higher order of industrial, social, and individual life.

THE END.

Printed by Cowan & Co, Limited, Perth.

OPINIONS OF THE PRESS

ON THE

SOCIAL SCIENCE SERIES.

"'The Principles of State Interference' is another of Messrs. Swan Sonnenschein's Series of Handbooks on Scientific Social Subjects. It would be fitting to close our remarks on this little work with a word of commendation of the publishers of so many useful volumes by eminent writers on questions of pressing interest to a large number of the community. We have now received and read a good number of the handbooks which Messrs. Swan Sonnenschein have published in this series, and can speak in the highest terms of them. They are written by men of considerable knowledge of the subjects they have undertaken to discuss; they are concise; they give a fair estimate of the progress which recent discussion has added towards the solution of the pressing social questions of to-day, are well up to date, and are published at a price within the resources of the public to which they are likely to be of the most use."—*Westminster Review*, July, 1891.

" The excellent 'Social Science Series,' which is published at as low a price as to place it within everybody's reach."—*Review of Reviews*.

' A most useful series. . . . This impartial series welcomes both just writers and unjust."—*Manchester Guardian*.

" Concise in treatment, lucid in style and moderate in price, these books can hardly fail to do much towards spreading sound views on economic and social questions."—*Review of the Churches*.

" Convenient, well-printed, and moderately-priced volumes."—*Reynold's Newspaper*.

" There is a certain impartiality about the attractive and well-printed volumes which form the series to which the works noticed in this article belong. There is no editor and no common design beyond a desire to redress those errors and irregularities of society which all the writers, though they may agree in little else, concur in acknowledging and deploring. The system adopted appears to be to select men known to have a claim to speak with more or less authority upon the shortcomings of civilisation, and to allow each to propound the views which commend themselves most strongly to his mind, without reference to the possible flat contradiction which may be forthcoming at the hands of the next contributor."—*Literary World*.

" 'The Social Science Series' aims at the illustration of all sides of social and economic truth and error."—*Scotsman*.

SWAN SONNENSCHEIN & CO., LONDON.

SOCIAL SCIENCE SERIES.

SCARLET CLOTH, EACH 2s. 6d.

1. **Work and Wages.**   Prof. J. E. THOROLD ROGERS.
   "Nothing that Professor Rogers writes can fail to be of interest to thoughtful people."—*Athenæum.*
2. **Civilisation: Its Cause and Cure.**   EDWARD CARPENTER.
   "No passing piece of polemics, but a permanent possession."—*Scottish Review.*
3. **Quintessence of Socialism.**   Dr. SCHÄFFLE.
   "Precisely the manual needed. Brief, lucid, fair and wise."—*British Weekly.*
4. **Darwinism and Politics.**   D. G. RITCHIE, M.A. (Oxon.).
   New Edition, with two additional Essays on HUMAN EVOLUTION.
   "One of the most suggestive books we have met with."—*Literary World.*
5. **Religion of Socialism.**   E. BELFORT BAX.
6. **Ethics of Socialism.**   E. BELFORT BAX.
   "Mr. Bax is by far the ablest of the English exponents of Socialism."—*Westminster Review.*
7. **The Drink Question.**   Dr. KATE MITCHELL.
   "Plenty of interesting matter for reflection.'—*Graphic.*
8. **Promotion of General Happiness.**   Prof. M. MACMILLAN.
   "A reasoned account of the most advanced and most enlightened utilitarian doctrine in a clear and readable form."—*Scotsman.*
9. **England's Ideal, &c.**   EDWARD CARPENTER.
   "The literary power is unmistakable, their freshness of style, their humour, and their enthusiasm."—*Pall Mall Gazette.*
10. **Socialism in England.**   SIDNEY WEBB, LL.B.
    "The best general view of the subject from the modern Socialist side."—*Athenæum.*
11. **Prince Bismarck and State Socialism.**   W. H. DAWSON.
    "A succinct, well-digested review of German social and economic legislation since 1870."—*Saturday Review.*
12. **Godwin's Political Justice (On Property).**   Edited by H. S. SALT.
    "Shows Godwin at his best; with an interesting and informing introduction."—*Glasgow Herald.*
13. **The Story of the French Revolution.**   E. BELFORT BAX.
    "A trustworthy outline."—*Scotsman.*
14. **The Co-Operative Commonwealth.**   LAURENCE GRONLUND.
    "An independent exposition of the Socialism of the Marx school."—*Contemporary Review.*
15. **Essays and Addresses.**   BERNARD BOSANQUET, M.A. (Oxon.).
    "Ought to be in the hands of every student of the Nineteenth Century spirit."—*Echo.*
    "No one can complain of not being able to understand what Mr. Bosanquet means."—*Pall Mall Gazette.*
16. **Charity Organisation.**   C. S. LOCH, Secretary to Charity Organisation Society.
    "A perfect little manual."—*Athenæum.*
    "Deserves a wide circulation."—*Scotsman.*
17. **Thoreau's Anti-Slavery and Reform Papers.**   Edited by H. S. SALT.
    "An interesting collection of essays."—*Literary World.*
18. **Self-Help a Hundred Years Ago.**   G. J. HOLYOAKE.
    "Will be studied with much benefit by all who are interested in the amelioration of the condition of the poor."—*Morning Post.*
19. **The New York State Reformatory at Elmira.**   ALEXANDER WINTER.
    With Preface by HAVELOCK ELLIS.
    "A valuable contribution to the literature of penology."—*Black and White.*

SOCIAL SCIENCE SERIES—(Continued).

20. **Common Sense about Women.** T. W. HIGGINSON.
"An admirable collection of papers, advocating in the most liberal spirit the emancipation of women." — *Woman's Herald.*

21. **The Unearned Increment.** W. H. DAWSON.
"A concise but comprehensive volume." — *Echo.*

22. **Our Destiny.** LAURENCE GRONLUND.
"A very vigorous little book, dealing with the influence of Socialism on morals and religion." — *Scotsman.*

23. **The Working-Class Movement in America.**
Dr EDWARD and E. MARX AVELING.
"Will give a good idea of the condition of the working classes in America, and of the various organisations which they have formed." — *Scots Leader.*

24. **Luxury.** Prof. EMILE DE LAVELEYE.
"An eloquent plea on moral and economical grounds for simplicity of life." — *Academy.*

25. **The Land and the Labourers.** Rev. C. W. STUBBS, M.A.
"This admirable book should be circulated in every village in the country." — *Manchester Guardian.*

26. **The Evolution of Property.** PAUL LAFARGUE.
"Will prove interesting and profitable to all students of economic history." — *Scotsman.*

27. **Crime and Its Causes.** W. DOUGLAS MORRISON.
"Can hardly fail to suggest to our readers several new and pregnant reflections on the subject." — *Anti-Jacobin.*

28. **Principles of State Interference.** D. G. RITCHIE, M.A.
"An interesting contribution to the controversy on the functions of the State." — *Glasgow Herald.*

29. **German Socialism and F. Lassalle.** W. H. DAWSON.
"As a biographical history of German Socialistic movements during this century it may be accepted as complete." — *British Weekly.*

30. **The Purse and the Conscience.** H. M. THOMPSON, B.A. (Cantab.).
"Shows common sense and fairness in his arguments." — *Scotsman.*

31. **Origin of Property in Land.** FUSTEL DE COULANGES. Edited, with an Introductory Chapter on the English Manor, by Prof. W. J. ASHLEY, M.A.
"His views are clearly stated, and are worth reading." — *Saturday Review.*

32. **The English Republic.** W. J. LINTON. Edited by KINETON PARKES.
"Characterised by that vigorous intellectuality which has marked his long life of literary and artistic activity." — *Glasgow Herald.*

33. **The Co-Operative Movement.** BEATRICE POTTER.
"Without doubt the ablest and most philosophical analysis of the Co-Operative Movement which has yet been produced." — *Speaker.*

34. **Neighbourhood Guilds.** Dr. STANTON COIT.
"A most suggestive little book to anyone interested in the social question." — *Pall Mall Gazette.*

35. **Modern Humanists.** J. M. ROBERTSON.
"Mr. Robertson's style is excellent—nay, even brilliant—and his purely literary criticisms bear the mark of much acumen." — *Times.*

36. **Outlooks from the New Standpoint.** E. BELFORT BAX.
"Mr. Bax is a very acute and accomplished student of history and economics." — *Daily Chronicle.*

37. **Distributing Co-Operative Societies.** Dr. LUIGI PIZZAMIGLIO. Edited by F. J. SNELL.
"Dr. Pizzamiglio has gathered together and grouped a wide array of facts and statistics, and they speak for themselves." — *Speaker.*

38. **Collectivism and Socialism.** By A. NAQUET. Edited by W. HEAFORD.
"An admirable criticism by a well known French politician of the New Socialism of Marx and Lassalle." — *Daily Chronicle.*

SOCIAL SCIENCE SERIES—(*Continued*).

39. **The London Programme.**   Sidney Webb, LL.B.
 "Brimful of excellent ideas."—*Anti-Jacobin.*
40. **The Modern State.**   Paul Leroy Beaulieu.
 "A most interesting book; well worth a place in the library of every social inquirer."—*N. B. Economist.*
41. **The Condition of Labour.**   Henry George.
 "Written with striking ability, and sure to attract attention."—*Newcastle Chronicle.*
42. **The Revolutionary Spirit preceding the French Revolution.**
 Felix Rocquain. With a Preface by Professor Huxley.
 "The student of the French Revolution will find in it an excellent introduction to the study of that catastrophe."—*Scotsman.*
43. **The Student's Marx.**   Edward Aveling, D.Sc.
 "One of the most practically useful of any in the Series."—*Glasgow Herald.*
44. **A Short History of Parliament.**   B. C. Skottowe, M.A. (Oxon.).
 "Deals very carefully and completely with this side of constitutional history."—*Spectator.*
45. **Poverty: Its Genesis and Exodus.**   J. G. Godard.
 "He states the problems with great force and clearness."—*N. B. Economist.*
46. **The Trade Policy of Imperial Federation.**   Maurice H. Hervey.
 "An interesting contribution to the discussion."—*Publishers' Circular.*
47. **The Dawn of Radicalism.**   J. Bowles Daly, LL.D.
 "Forms an admirable picture of an epoch more pregnant, perhaps, with political instruction than any other in the world's history."—*Daily Telegraph.*
48. **The Destitute Alien in Great Britain.** Arnold White; Montague Crackanthorpe, Q.C.; W. A. M'Arthur, M.P.; W. H. Wilkins, &c.
 "Much valuable information concerning a burning question of the day."—*Times.*
49. **Illegitimacy and the Influence of Seasons on Conduct.**
 Albert Leffingwell, M.D.
 "We have not often seen a work based on statistics which is more continuously interesting."—*Westminster Review.*
50. **Commercial Crises of the Nineteenth Century.**   H. M. Hyndman.
 "One of the best and most permanently useful volumes of the Series."—*Literary Opinion.*
51. **The State and Pensions in Old Age.** J. A. Spender and Arthur Acland, M.P.
 "A careful and cautious examination of the question."—*Times.*
52. **The Fallacy of Saving.**   John M. Robertson.
 "A plea for the reorganisation of our social and industrial system."—*Speaker.*
53. **The Irish Peasant.**   Anon.
 "A real contribution to the Irish Problem by a close, patient and dispassionate investigator."—*Daily Chronicle.*
54. **The Effects of Machinery on Wages.**   Prof. J. S. Nicholson, D.Sc.
 "Ably reasoned, clearly stated, impartially written."—*Literary World.*
55. **The Social Horizon.**   Anon.
 "A really admirable little book, bright, clear, and unconventional."—*Daily Chronicle.*
56. **Socialism, Utopian and Scientific.**   Frederick Engels.
 "The body of the book is still fresh and striking."—*Daily Chronicle.*
57. **Land Nationalisation.**   A. R. Wallace.
 "The most instructive and convincing of the popular works on the subject."—*National Reformer.*
58. **The Ethic of Usury and Interest.**   Rev. W. Blissard.
 "The work is marked by genuine ability."—*North British Agriculturalist.*
59. **The Emancipation of Women.**   Adele Crepaz.
 "By far the most comprehensive, luminous, and penetrating work on this question that I have yet met with."—*Extract from Mr.* Gladstone's *Preface.*
60. **The Eight Hours' Question.**   John M. Robertson.

DOUBLE VOLUMES, Each 3s. 6d.

1. **Life of Robert Owen.**   Lloyd Jones.
2. **The Impossibility of Social Democracy: a Second Part of "The Quintessence of Socialism".**   Dr. A. Schäffle.
3. **The Condition of the Working Class in England in 1844.** Frederick Engels.
4. **The Principles of Social Economy.**   Yves Guyot.

www.ingramcontent.com/pod-product-compliance
Lightning Source LLC
Chambersburg PA
CBHW022116160426
43197CB00009B/1050